WE ARE THE LEGION

Julie Summers

WE ARE THE LEGION

The Royal British Legion at 100

PROFILE
EDITIONS

ROYAL BRITISH LEGION

100 YEARS OF SUPPORTING THE ARMED
FORCES COMMUNITY

CONTENTS

WINDSOR CASTLE

On the centenary of its formation, I send my heartfelt congratulations to the Royal British Legion at home and overseas, and commend its one hundred years of service to the Armed Forces community.

Since 1921, when four ex-service organisations joined together in a spirit of placing service to others before self, the Legion has worked with alacrity, intelligence and commitment, pursuing a mission of bringing together nations, communities and people to provide better futures for our Armed Forces, veterans and their families.

Remarkably, the Legion's purpose has remained unchanged to this day, as it continues to provide help and assistance to the Armed Forces community under a lifelong duty of care, whilst keeping its promise never to forget the service and sacrifice of those who have been prepared to step into harm's way, in defence of democracy and freedom.

As you reflect on your long history and consider your future, I have pleasure in sending all those associated with the Royal British Legion my best wishes on this very special anniversary.

ELIZABETH R

7

LIEUTENANT GENERAL JAMES BASHALL CB CBE
National President

The Royal British Legion has been a constant presence in the life of the United Kingdom since its inception 100 years ago. Born out of the aftermath of the First World War, it has fulfilled its duty of care to the Armed Forces community with compassion, resourcefulness, energy and intelligence. It has led from the front in the best interests of those unique individuals prepared to step in harm's way in defence of their Queen and country.

Formed as an amalgamation of four organisations, each focused on returning Servicemen's needs from the First World War, the Legion represents the national lead on Remembrance across the nation. It also has a commitment to hold the government of the day to account on behalf of those who were prepared to pay the ultimate price for our freedom. Over the years it has fought for better pensions for veterans and war widows. It has campaigned for the fair treatment of those disabled by war, whether physically or mentally. It is the organisation at the heart of national Remembrance. It honours the memory of all those who have died in the service of their country, and the contribution of all those who serve or have served in Her Majesty's Armed Forces.

The Royal British Legion is a military charity with membership branches and area offices across England, Wales and Northern Ireland, while north of the border our support services are delivered through Poppyscotland, a part of the Legion group of charities. We also have membership branches overseas, in territories as far flung as Gibraltar and Hong Kong. Our members, whose motto is 'Service not Self', provide companionship, keep Remembrance, and work for those in the Armed Forces community who are in need. Our early founders, who came together in May 1921 to put aside the differences between their four organisations and to work in unity for their community, would be proud to think that the Legion has had such an active history over the last century. They would also understand that there is still work to be done. Our strong message is that we will continue to look after the interests of the Armed Forces community and honour the service and sacrifice of all who serve or have served in the British Armed Forces.

UNA CLEMINSON BEM TD
National Chairman

For the past 100 years members of the Royal British Legion have kept faith with the early founders' commitment to the Armed Forces community of serving personnel, veterans and their dependants. Formed out of the ashes of the First World War, the Legion has had to adapt and develop over a century that has seen a further world war and many other conflicts. Throughout, the Legion has been there to create better lives for Service and ex-Service personnel and their families.

This book tells the story not only of those influential men and women who steered the course of the Legion over the years but also of the ordinary people who are the lifeblood of the organisation. It covers the well-known aspects of the Legion's public work – the Poppy Appeals, Remembrance Sundays and the Festivals of Remembrance at the Royal Albert Hall – and it also looks at the behind-the-scenes work that goes on; to help those who are in need, to campaign in their interest, and to honour their service and sacrifice.

The Royal British Legion has people at its heart. It campaigns nationally for the Service and veterans' community and it takes seriously its commitment to be able to reach every town and village where help is required. With its network of branches around the world, it has responsibility for every ex-Serviceman or woman who has been a part of the British Armed Forces, whether in the world wars or in more recent conflicts. Wherever the Legion is found, it also remembers and pays tribute to all those who have fought at Britain's side from the UK and Commonwealth forces, including other nation's forces who have served under British command.

I hope you will enjoy reading this book and that it inspires you to join us in creating a land fit for heroes in our second century of service to the Armed Forces community.

INTRODUCTION

When the Canadian singer and poet Leonard Cohen released *Various Positions* in December 1984 no one could have predicted that one of the songs on the album would become a worldwide hit. 'Hallelujah' has gone through many iterations since that time and has been covered by scores of artists. There have been stand-out performances of it too. But perhaps none so emotionally charged as the one at the Royal Albert Hall on 10 November 2018 when Sheku Kanneh-Mason played it, accompanied by the Countess of Wessex's String Orchestra. Hauntingly beautiful, the cello's voice rose and swelled as the orchestra subtly joined in the melody. During the third verse, 100 men, women and children walked onto the floor of the great hall and stood in an oval with their backs to the cellist. Each held a photograph of a family member who had died in the First World War. Then 5,500 people in the audience rose to their feet, each holding a picture of a man who had lost his life in the war. The whole scene was projected in black and white, a powerful reminder of the passage of time since each of those young men, and millions more on both sides of the conflict, had died.

Sheku Kanneh-Mason was just 19 when he played at the Royal British Legion's Festival of Remembrance. He had been named the BBC Young Musician of the Year in 2016, the first black musician to be awarded the

honour, and earlier in 2018 had played three pieces at the wedding of Prince Harry and Meghan Markle. When asked what it had been like to play at the festival he replied: 'It was a very moving and emotional occasion for me. I wanted to bear witness to the sad loss of life of so many particularly young men who were so close to my age. Playing Leonard Cohen's "Hallelujah" was my way of expressing a sense of tragedy, sorrow and prayer.' On the 100th anniversary of the end of the First World War there can hardly have been a more fitting gesture of respect and remembrance.

Watched by millions around the globe, the Legion's annual Festival of Remembrance is a magnificent display of military drills from all three branches of the Armed Forces, with music from military bands and civilian musicians. Initially intended as an event

to honour those lost in the First World War it now remembers those who lost their lives in the Second World War and subsequent conflicts. The parade of Servicemen and women is the culmination of the festival and this includes representatives from youth organisations and uniformed public security services of the City of London.

The festival's brilliant choreography, its proud military bearing and its moving traditions, including the dropping of a million poppies during the muster, stand in stark contrast to the chaos, grief and tragedy that lurked in Britain in the aftermath of that terrible war. It was out of the debris and rot of four years of trench warfare that the organisation now known as the Royal British Legion was born in 1921. The Legion is on the public's radar around Remembrancetide and is

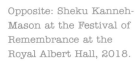

Opposite: Sheku Kanneh-Mason at the Festival of Remembrance at the Royal Albert Hall, 2018.

Right: Members of the Band of Her Majesty's Royal Marines, Royal Albert Hall, 2019.

Above: Leon Parker struggled to cope leaving the army after 4½ years. He says without the support of the Legion 'I dread to think what might have happened'.

inextricably linked with the poppy, the national symbol of Remembrance and hope for a peaceful future, but it is active all year round, supporting members of the Armed Forces and veterans whose needs are often complex and urgent. This is the story of the first 100 years of the Legion's history.

THE ROYAL BRITISH LEGION

Today the Royal British Legion is Britain's largest military charity with a membership of 220,000 spread over 2,500 branches in the UK and a further 78 worldwide. Larger than the next four military charities combined, it has standing with government and a huge reach into the community it serves. At its core are people, individuals who have at their hearts the well-being of the Armed Forces community. The branch system has been in place since the inception of the British Legion in May 1921 and is a great strength. With a footprint in almost every town and many villages across the four countries of the United Kingdom, branches are ideally placed to spot welfare needs locally and bring them to the attention of the wider Legion. Away from the public gaze of the glitter of the festival and the pathos of Remembrance, the Legion acts quietly but with determination to ensure that anyone who has served in the British Armed Forces is not disadvantaged by his or her Service.

Over the first century of its existence much changed for the Legion. Since the end of the Second World War Britain has had a welfare state, and the Armed Forces are no longer conscripted but comprise a professional body with a fraction of the number of Servicemen and women who served in the two world wars. The Legion began its life as an organisation that needed

to be called into existence to answer an immediate need, namely to provide help, care and welfare for the millions of returning Servicemen and their families, dependants, widows and orphans who struggled to cope in the aftermath of the most destructive war in history to date. Over the years many of those needs, either immediate or longer-term, were met but the fundamentals of the Legion's role have not gone away.

Today the Legion's mission is the same as it was in 1921: Remembrance, welfare and campaigning. That has not changed but the way the Legion delivers on it has, and that is the result of decades of hard work and professional development. In the early days and up to the end of the 20th century, care services were delivered by the Legion in the field, at branch level. The Legion provided a great spread of help but as needs became more complex, with an ageing population and different sorts of issues for the 21st-century Armed Forces community, it became necessary to move towards more professional and targeted provision. Today the Legion looks to experts to deliver specialist care when needed, while continuing to offer welfare assistance through its branches and their trained volunteers.

Remembrance too has changed since the first Armistice Day service in 1919. Today the Legion has a network countrywide that works with communities, schools and youth groups, as well as with veterans, to keep the Act of Remembrance alive. The sight of Legion Standard Bearers at war memorials and in places of worship is so familiar that it has become part of the fabric of our society. The Legion is at the heart of modern Remembrance, as it has been for a century, and it continues to emphasise the importance and relevance of this on a year-round basis. This

Top: London Poppy Day, 2018.

Above: A marcher on parade at the 2020 Cenotaph service in the dress of the Gurkha Logistic Regiment.

is particularly successful at the National Memorial Arboretum in Staffordshire which is the nation's centre of Remembrance.

Campaigning for returning Service personnel and their dependants was at the core of what the Legion did in the early 1920s. Although great strides were made over the 20th century there is no room for complacency. War pensions, widows' pensions, and benefits for veterans from all conflicts are constantly under review by both government and the Legion. The relationship between the state and the Legion is one that needs constantly to be maintained so that the Legion's commitment to the Armed Forces community is upheld.

This book falls into eight chapters, each focusing on a different aspect of the Legion's work over the last 100 years. It shows how much has changed in terms of care for Service personnel and veterans physically and mentally damaged by conflict. It will remind the reader how the Legion continues to honour and remember service and sacrifice and of its campaigning in the interests of the Armed Forces and veterans. It will also show that in some areas not enough has changed and the needs of those who call on the Legion are the same as the needs of their forebears. Sometimes the Legion is directly involved; at other times it operates at arm's length. At all times it aims to be there for those who need it most. This book does not promise to be a complete history but rather offers stories aimed at bringing the Legion to life.

Opposite: Doug Farrington, aged 93, one of 255 D-Day veterans aboard the MV *Boudicca*, June 2019.

Right: Sea cadets mark Remembrance Sunday in Carrickfergus, Northern Ireland, 2012.

Chapter 1

WHO FIRED THE STARTING GUN?

Above: Ex-soldiers offering services on the street were a common but distressing sight.

Before the First World War a returning soldier could expect little in the way of support apart from a small war pension. He was abandoned to fortune, or destitution. With a civilian volunteer (later conscripted) army, navy and flying corps (later the Royal Air Force) comprising millions of men fighting for Britain and its Empire, this was no longer possible. During the war, the British government set up a scheme whereby men who returned to Britain through injury could claim compensation. While it gave with the one hand it took away with the other. Such was the shortage of fighting-fit men that some who had been through the medical system were sent back to the front line. These included men who were medically unfit to serve.

The injustice of this led to the formation in January 1917 of a body called the National Federation of Discharged and Demobilized Sailors and Soldiers whose slogan was 'Every man once before any man twice'. The Federation was based in the south-east of England and had affiliation to the Liberal Party. The National Association of Discharged Sailors and Soldiers was formed in Blackburn the same year. It had strong links to the Labour Party and campaigned for better pensions. A third body, also formed in 1917, was the Comrades of the Great War, which came into being to fight for the rights of the ex-Serviceman and woman.

Top: Men waiting to sign on for unemployment benefits, 1922.

Above: Ex-Servicemen protesting on behalf of thousands who had lost jobs, c.1923.

After the war was over one of the most pressing issues that the three bodies of the Federation, Association and Comrades had to face was the chaos of demobilisation. So-called 'key workers' were released first as they were considered vital to get industry up and running again, which caused a great deal of resentment among those who had been in the Services for longer. As far back as 1917 Field Marshal Haig had made plans for the end of the war and proposed demobilisation based on age and length of Service. His suggestion met with little sympathy in the War Cabinet at the time and it was only when Winston Churchill became Secretary of State for War in 1919 that the memorandum resurfaced and Churchill asked why nothing had been done about it.

By 1919 the army was experiencing turmoil. In London, France and elsewhere demonstrations took place. There were riots by serving soldiers who were deeply angered by the way demobilisation was being handled. This gave rise to concern in Britain that there would be civil unrest. The government feared a Bolshevik-style revolution, but the Federation, Association and Comrades campaigned against the revolutionary propaganda and were credited with helping to head off a dangerous situation.

Haig, who had refused to be associated with any one of the ex-Service organisations as they existed separately, could see that what was required was a unifying influence. It was clear to him that there should be one large, non-political organisation that represented all ranks of the Armed Forces, including officers, that would hold the government to account on behalf of the men and women it represented. By spring 1920 the Federation and the Comrades had realised that unity was the only way forward and

FIELD MARSHAL DOUGLAS HAIG, FIRST EARL HAIG KT, GCB, OM, GCVO, KCIE

Of the men involved in the early years of the Royal British Legion, Field Marshal Earl Haig stands out as the most influential. Lionised by the men who served under him both during and after the war, he was a popular founder President and devoted himself with great energy to the welfare of ex-Servicemen from the end of the war until his sudden death in January 1928 at the age of 66.

At the outbreak of the First World War Major General Douglas Haig was in command of the First Army of the British Expeditionary Force. By the end of 1915 he was appointed Commander-in-Chief of the British Army, a position he held until the end of the war. His role in the First World War received much scrutiny and criticism in the middle years of the 20th century but at the time the British Legion was founded he was considered to be the greatest military leader in the country.

Haig's concern for the future of the men who had served Britain in France, Belgium and further afield began before the war had ended. Over the course of the next seven years he worked tirelessly for the Legion, launching the Poppy Day Appeal in 1921 and helping to shape modern Remembrance. But he also worked hard at grass-roots level, touring the country with Lady Haig, visiting branches, opening bowling greens and hospital wards. As a personality he could come across as removed. This was probably on account of his shyness and the mores of the era in which he grew up, but he was often visibly moved by the plight of some of the men and women he encountered on his travels.

Haig formed the British Empire Services League in 1921 and encouraged mutual support and understanding between those who had fought together. This lives on in the form of the Royal Commonwealth Ex-Services League, conducting its welfare work in poorer parts of the Commonwealth from its offices at the Royal British Legion, which supports its work.

On 27 January 1928 Haig made a scheduled visit to the Poppy Factory in Richmond and greeted a group of scouts. The next day he was dead. It was a devastating loss to the Legion. Haig's commitment had earned him the undying devotion of its members. Whatever brickbats were thrown at his reputation they would not ignore the fact that he was a man who always put duty before self.

they called a conference to which they invited other organisations, including the Officers' Association and a revolutionary group called the National Union of Ex-Servicemen, known as NUX. The conference was chaired by Fred Lister, president of the Federation, who turned out to be unremitting, determined and outstandingly deft at heading off arguments.

On Sunday 15 May 1921, a wet and dreary day, a small number of ex-Servicemen walked to the Cenotaph war memorial in London's Whitehall. As Big Ben struck nine, four men representing societies that for three years had been rivals laid a wreath at the base of the memorial. On that wreath were the badges of the four organisations that would officially amalgamate to form the British Legion. It had taken months of talks, the energy and calibre of Earl Haig and the negotiating skills of Fred Lister to bring together four bodies, all focused on the care for ex-Servicemen, their widows and orphans, to agree to unite in the widest possible interest of the ex-Service community.

Fred Lister wrote of this energy in the first edition of the Legion's monthly magazine the *Journal* in July 1921: 'The part that the British Legion will play in the nation will be decided by the branches of the Legion. The Legion is a body which will give to the individual ex-Service man, without regard to his war rank, an opportunity of serving his country in order that the victory of 1918 may have been worth the sacrifice.'

The following day the constitution was presented to and agreed upon by 700 delegates from all over Britain at the Unity Conference in London. On that momentous occasion the Prince of Wales was invited to become the British Legion's first Patron, which he accepted. Earl Haig was to be its first President and Lister the National Chairman, this last

being greeted with cheers of acclamation. Colonel George Crosfield was elected Vice Chairman and Major Brunel Cohen MP was to become Honorary Treasurer. A demonstration of the new organisation's attitude towards its members was shown when the constitution was proposed by a soldier and seconded by a general. There would be no distinction between rank, religion or political affiliation. This was something the press picked up on, as they did on the commitment to a non-political stance, which they applauded.

THE JOURNAL FOR ALL EX-SERVICE MEN. PRICE 3ᵈ MONTHLY

BRITISH LEGION

With which is incorporated the Comrades' Journal and the DSS Bulletin

Right: Front cover of the first edition of the monthly *Journal*, July 1921.

THE COLD REALITY

After the euphoria and excitement of the birth of the Legion came the reality of what the founding members were faced with. More than 6 million men from Britain had served during the First World War, of whom more than 700,000 were killed and some 1.75 million wounded or disabled. Of that latter number more than half were permanently disabled. Widows, orphans, families of the wounded, disabled and unemployed all needed the Legion's support. At that stage, the Legion estimated it had responsibility for up to 20 million people.

The first four years of the Legion's existence coincided with the economic hangover from the war, followed by the Great Depression. It was a time of mass unemployment and great uncertainty. Before the war Britain had been the world's leading trading and lending nation. British merchandise imports and exports were almost a third larger than Germany's and

Left: Poverty was a major issue for the Legion in the 1920s. Large families occupied back-to-back houses in towns and cities throughout the country, as here in Birmingham.

Opposite, left: The Poppy Fund helps to feed children in Crouch End, 1922.

half again as those of the United States. The City of London was the world's leading financial centre.

Where once Britain had dominated world markets, it now found it had rivals. As it had withdrawn from South Africa and South America to concentrate manufacture on the war effort, so Japan and the United States had stepped in to fill the gap as demand remained. Automation in manufacturing had begun to replace skilled workers and many men found themselves out of work. People in Britain wanted to return to the pre-war way of life, but Britain's financial position was weak. Her foreign assets had been run down at the same time as government debt had been run up. The stark reality was that 19th-century policy frameworks met 20th-century circumstances and the result was uncomfortable.

The first slump came in 1921 when unemployment rose to 2 million out of a population of 42 million. One of the many problems was that young men who had volunteered or been conscripted into the Armed Forces had missed out on up to four years of work, training or education. This was to be a running sore for years

The Legion's first Chairman, Thomas Frederick Lister, was an insurance agent who, in 1914, volunteered for Service in the Royal Garrison Artillery as a lance-bombardier. He was 28 years old and six feet six inches tall (198cm) at a time when the average height of a man was a whole foot (30cm) shorter. In 1916 he was badly wounded and discharged from the Army. Once back in Britain, he showed remarkable energy in fighting for national recognition of the plight of the veterans of the First World War. He became an important figure in the British former Service movement, chairing the National Federation of Discharged and Demobilized Sailors and Soldiers. His height reinforced his presence, but it was his intelligence and ability to think clearly and quickly that made him stand out.

Although only in his early thirties when he took on the chairmanship of the Unity Conference and later the Legion, he was not only unafraid of speaking his mind to men many years his senior, but he was also unfazed by those above him in rank. He told men in later years that they should not be afraid of opposing older men.

After he retired from the role in 1927, Lister remained an active member of the Legion's National Executive until his death in 1966. He championed the Legion's rehabilitation scheme, which aimed to provide homes for ex-Servicemen after the Second World War. Lister was created a CBE in 1927 and was knighted in 1961. Many thought the honour was long overdue.

Over the six years Lister served as Chairman, the Legion developed from a fledgling organisation into an established part of British life. His firm, guiding hand and his ability to deal with dissent graciously were key to that success.

Above: The *British Legion Album*, compiled annually with contributions from artists, musicians and endorsements from the Royal Family, was sold to raise funds.

to come. Another issue was the change in industry in Britain. New players had entered the fray – chemicals, vehicles and hosiery – expanding employment in those areas, but at the same time the traditional industries such as ship building, coal and cotton declined by a larger percentage. Workers from the old industries found it difficult to adapt to the new either because of the skills required or because of location. Areas of the UK were affected in different ways. In London and the south-east, average unemployment between 1923 and 1938 was 8 per cent. For the same period in Wales and Northern Ireland it was 22 per cent, while in the coal-mining areas it ran at 23 per cent and in the metal trades it was 24 per cent. One in three of the unemployed was an ex-Serviceman.

A major concern for the Legion in the early days was money. To carry out the work it had committed to would require vast sums. From November 1921 it ran annual Poppy Day Appeals and these provided the majority of its income. The money raised from the first Poppy Day Appeal in November 1921, which will be examined in the next chapter, was £84,000 (£4 million in today's money) after costs had been deducted. It was a good start, but it was not enough. The job for the Legion was to establish a balance between philanthropy and self-help. It was summed up by the Chairman, Lister, as the sword and the shield approach. The Legion did not have the resources to offer universal help, that was the role of government, but it was, and remains there, for real hardship cases and also as a vehicle to facilitate self-help in whatever form is of the most use.

As well as raising money and helping those in need, the Legion had other obligations under its charter. The overarching premise is that the Armed Forces will not fail the nation and the nation will not fail the Armed

Forces. This is known as the Armed Forces Covenant which the Legion championed at the outset and was to champion again nearly 90 years later, reviving the sense of mutual obligation during conflicts in Iraq and Afghanistan. One of its key roles was to lobby for better pension and disability provision for those who had been injured, disabled, widowed or orphaned as a result of active Service. It still has that role today. Another was to work hard for peace and to ensure that war on the scale of that witnessed in 1914–18 would never happen again. This was a sincere hope held not only by the Legion but by international ex-Servicemen's organisations all over the world. During the interwar years, the Legion was actively committed to working with ex-enemy organisations.

The Legion is the only military charity in Britain that has branches with members. Once the national body was formed, it was down to areas to set up local branches. This they did with astonishing energy. By the end of the first year Lister was able to write in the *Journal* that 2,500 branches had been established. That rose to over 4,750 at its peak in the 1950s and stands at 2,500 today plus a small but active number abroad, reminding us that the Legion was born out of the need to care for everyone who fought in the war including the members of the then Empire. Today it has reach across the Commonwealth with branches in places as far away as the Falkland Islands and Hong Kong.

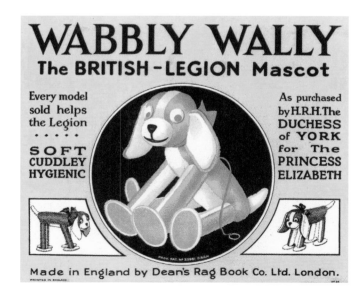

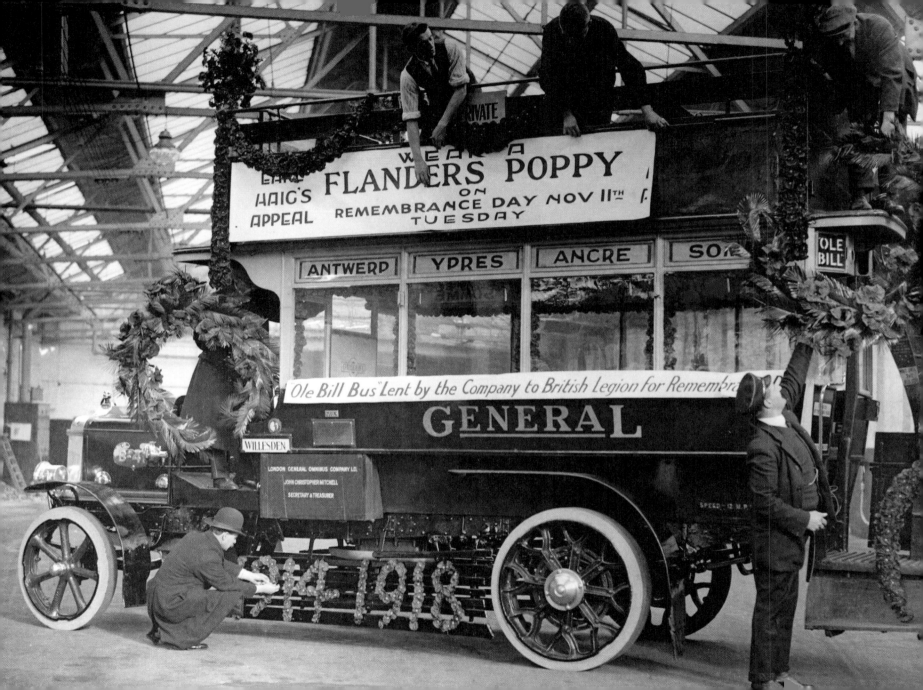

British Legion
663463
SUPPLIED BY
BIRMINGHAM MEDAL CO. LTD.
MEDALLISTS & BADGE MAKERS
BIRMINGHAM

NOTICE.

This Badge remains the property of the British Legion and is returnable under Rule 3 (D) of the Royal Charter.

Opposite: 'Ole Bill' was a First World War bus, decorated for Remembrance Day 1924. It was taken out of retirement in the 1970s to inspire a new generation to give generously to the Poppy Appeal.

Left and below: British Legion pin badges, like this original from the late 1920s, were popular with the public and advertised in the *Journal*.

LEGIONAIRES
Wear your Badge

OBTAINABLE AT
YOUR OWN BRANCH

HONORARY MEMBERS' BADGE
1/- each
**
TIE PINS or PENDANTS
1/- each

ORDINARY MEMBERS' BADGE
1/- each
**
CUFF LINKS
2/6 per pair

Printed by The Press Printers, Ltd., 69–76, Long Acre, W.C.2, and published monthly by the National Executive Council, British Legion. All communications upon Editorial or Business matters to be addressed to The British Legion, 26, Eccleston Square, S.W.1.

ENTER THE WOMEN

In a speech in Leicester in 1920, Earl Haig spoke of the need to enlist the support of women. Initially they could not become members of the Legion itself, so they formed the Women's Section in July 1921. The war had consumed a vast amount of female labour both at home and abroad. The munitions industry had a female workforce numbering hundreds of thousands.

The history of the Women's Section is a colourful one and there have been times when harmony between it and the Legion has not been complete. In the early days there were still men who were suspicious of women and some made it difficult for Women's Section branches to be set up in their area. In 1924 Earl Haig wrote to the chairman of every Legion branch urging support for the Women's Section. It was an issue that rumbled on in the background and caused quite a bit of ill-feeling at local level. The Women's Section has always had a royal patron. The longest serving was Her Majesty, Queen Elizabeth The Queen Mother, who accepted the position in 1924 and remained in that role until her death in 2002. She was succeeded by Her Royal Highness Anne, Princess Royal, who is a popular and active patron.

Over the last 100 years the role of the Women's Section has evolved but the fundamentals have not changed. It exists today to help women and children who find their welfare needs are not met by other services. One of its greatest commitments is to help children of serving and ex-Service personnel to get the best from their education. This can start with pre-school assistance for the purchase of baby items, essential clothing, bedroom furniture and school equipment and can lead to travel grants and, in some cases, school fees.

Below, left: Her Majesty, Queen Elizabeth's broadcast to women of the world from Buckingham Palace on 11 November 1939.

Below, right: Standard Bearers from the Women's Section at the annual service at St Anne's, Westminster, 1934.

Opposite: The Duchess of York, later Queen Elizabeth, speaking at the British Legion conference, 1933.

POPPYSCOTLAND

Although the Legion had hoped to reach north of the border, events in Scotland had developed in a different direction in the summer of 1921. At first it was known as the Legion in Scotland and undertook much of the same work as the London-based Legion did in England, Wales and on the island of Ireland. By 1926 Edinburgh had Lady Haig's Poppy Factory and the Appeal was named the Earl Haig Fund (Scotland). This was registered as a distinct charity on 26 November 1956. Fifty years later the Earl Haig Fund (Scotland) adopted the trading name Poppyscotland, and a new year-round fundraising programme was launched.

In June 2011 Poppyscotland merged with the Royal British Legion. Under the terms of the merger additional investment has been committed to Scotland to make improvements to the support services for veterans and their families living north of the border. Poppyscotland continues to operate as a distinct, separate charity within the Royal British Legion group of charities. The Poppyscotland brand continues unchanged and the Scottish Poppy and Scottish Poppy Appeal remain in place, with funds raised from the campaign being used exclusively to support the Armed Forces and veterans' community living in Scotland.

Opposite: Chelsea Pensioners John Hellewell (left) and Barrie Davey on a visit to the Lady Haig Poppy Factory in Edinburgh, November 2018.

Top, right: Lady Haig during a presentation, 1918.

Right: Entrance gates to Panmure Close, Edinburgh, former home of Lady Haig's Poppy Factory.

A RETURN TO ARMS

As the 1930s wore on it became increasingly obvious to everyone in Britain that the world was facing the prospect of another major European, possibly world, war. It became a reality on 3 September 1939 and was to last for almost six years. That year, at the Women's Section annual conference, the Honorary Treasurer, Major Brunel Cohen, told the delegates how the 1938 Poppy Day Appeal funds had been distributed.

Almost £600,000 (£40 million) had been spent by the welfare teams on sick and distressed individuals. He also pointed out there were still 10,000 homeless ex-Servicemen, a number that shocked conference. It was clear there was still much for the Legion to do.

The Second World War was different from the First World War in many ways. It was a mobile conflict with new weapons and new horrors but with the same devastating consequences for those caught up in the fighting. This time it was total war, meaning one in which there were no non-combatants, and there was widespread bombing of towns and cities, killing thousands of civilians. Almost everyone was affected by some aspect of the Second World War and by its end the worldwide death toll had exceeded that of the First World War, though in terms of casualties the overall number of deaths in Britain and of British and Commonwealth Servicemen and women was lower than in 1914–18. Men and women returned broken in body and spirit by their experiences.

When called upon to help a new generation of ex-Service personnel, who swelled the existing number of people it was responsible for, the Legion was ready. Fred Lister had been appointed Chairman of the Legion's post-war planning committee to avoid the difficulties and mistakes of the years immediately after the Great War, and in order to study the whole problem of demobilisation and resettlement. The committee came up with a nine-point plan that addressed many of the issues that had been such a trial for those returning after the previous war. A key concern was men who had left their homes and civilian occupations to fight for their country and who had missed out on opportunities of advancement. The committee argued that they should be the first to be employed, not as a favour

Left: Londoners made homeless in the Blitz, October 1940.

Below, left: A family
evicted from their home in
Lambeth, 1937.

Below, right: British
Legion food depot at
Clapham Junction, 1932.
At this stage the Legion's
primary concern was
relief from distress.

but as an act of restitution. This time the government listened and the Legion took credit for two acts passed by the government regarding employment, one to make it obligatory to employ a certain number of ex-Servicemen and another to guarantee reinstatement into pre-war employment.

On the subject of pensions, the Legion succeeded in persuading the Attlee government 'to put the onus in cases of entitlement to pension on the State – an achievement of the greatest importance'. It had earlier secured legislation making compulsory the employment of a percentage of disabled men. This was another triumph and something that the Legion had been arguing for since 1921. The plan also included provision for fit men to enter academic and technical training for those who had had their studies disrupted by the war.

Nevertheless, the dislocation in the immediate post-war years was immense, the shortage of affordable housing extreme and the issue of employment a serious worry. Men who had been away from home for up to six years returned to families who had themselves endured bombing and death. Children had grown up, wives had gained independence and homes had changed or been lost. It was a difficult period of adjustment for families all over the country and it took months, years in some cases, to resolve.

The men from the Second World War who joined the Legion were known as 'this-war men' and were encouraged to take an active part in its running at local

and national level. There was a new energy from this cohort, who were prepared to stand up for the rights of those less fortunate than themselves. They argued, for example, that it was an ungrateful government that gave a disabled man a pension and expected him to be content with a life of inactivity and boredom. They wanted those men to have the chance to do meaningful work, not just jobs as caretakers or road sweepers.

After the introduction of the Welfare State in 1948 there were some who believed the Legion would become redundant as the government had stepped in to take over the areas of responsibility that the Legion had previously covered. The new National Health Service did mean that there were fewer calls on the Legion's benevolence. It no longer had to help buy surgical appliances, deaf aids or artificial limbs, but there were other, new, calls on its funds and the Legion was determined not to let anyone go in need if it had money in the bank. In fact the Legion's work expanded greatly after the Second World War as the 4.6 million returning ex-Service personnel tried to find work and adjust to life in the post-war world.

Over the course of the next 45 years the Legion continued to support the Armed Forces community, helping individuals to find employment and working with those injured in the service of their country in the Second World War and subsequent conflicts. One of the greatest areas of change was in the age of the beneficiaries. Women and men who were involved in the early years were now reaching their seventies and the need for care homes rather than holiday homes grew exponentially. By 1950 the Legion owned and ran four convalescent homes, where ex-Service personnel could stay after hospital treatment,

June 13 1945 — PUNCH *or The*

"This blessed plot, this earth, this realm, this England,..."

Great words—and true to-day, as in Elizabeth's time. Great men too, in her time, and ours, whose courage and sacrifices have preserved our freedom, our right to live at peace.

Let us praise them by thanking them—by generous aid to the British Legion, our greatest organisation dedicated to the rehabilitation of our fighting men. Comradeship born of service is perpetuated by 4,413 Legion Branches. 3,928 Centres give speedy aid in distress. For the disabled there are Legion workshops, teaching new trades and self-reliance; a housing scheme for family men. Legion Sanatoria aid the tuberculous—Preston Hall for men, Nayland Hall for women. A pensions scheme for the prematurely aged; weekly allowances in chronic sickness; advice and skilled advocacy in manifold pensions problems; an employment organisation for the workless. Training and upbringing of orphaned and physically handicapped children.

ALL these and many other friendly aids are offered to ex-Service men and women of ALL ranks and ALL Services, and their families, whether they are Legion members or not. This great work calls for the generous sympathy of all.

EARL HAIG'S APPEAL FUND

Gifts and legacies will be gratefully received, carefully applied. The address is:
HAIG'S FUND, RICHMOND, SURREY

BRITISH LEGION
PATRON H.M. THE KING

This space given by the proprietors of 'Ovaltine'

and four country homes that provided permanent residence for older and less mobile veterans. Twenty-five years later the country homes were still a vital part of the Legion's offering to the ageing population and today there are six nursing homes that cater for some 500 residents who receive professional nursing and dementia care. These homes have a staff of 750 with a further 400 volunteers who help to keep them running. The specialist nursing, dementia and end-of-life care delivered in these homes is of the highest quality but what visitors notice most is the wonderful atmosphere. The common bond of Service banter and humour is a marked feature of the Legion's homes.

The Legion's worldwide reach has always been key to its role in the Commonwealth. In the early days every country that had sent men to fight with the British Armed Forces had one or more branches and their duties were the same as in the UK: to look out for the welfare of ex-Servicemen and their families. Almost three million men from the then British Empire, colonies and dominions served with the British Army in the First World War.

All these were part of the Legion family in the post-war era. This far-flung membership represents Britain's past role as an imperial power and its Commonwealth ties.

Opposite: Earl Haig Appeal Fund poster, June 1945.

Left: Poster to encourage Servicemen and women from the Second World War to join the Legion.

THE DULMIAL GUN

In 1925 a ceremony was held in the village of Dulmial, in what was then India, to unveil a 19th-century 12-pounder cannon that had been given as a gift by the British. This was at the request of the village's highest-ranking and most decorated soldier, Captain Ghulam Mohammad Malik. He had been offered a gift of his choice as a thank you for the outstanding support offered by Dulmial in supplying the largest number of men to the British Army of any small village in undivided India. He chose the cannon for the village over money or land.

In 1914 there were some 870 men living in Dulmial. Men from the village had supported the British since the Indian Mutiny in 1857 and fought side by side with the British Army in the Second Afghan-Anglo War of the late 1870s, including Captain Ghulam Mohammad Malik

himself. At the outbreak of the First World War 460 men – almost every fit and able-bodied man – joined the British Army, of whom all but nine would return to Dulmial.

Twenty years later their assistance was requested again. By this time the village had expanded and 732 men volunteered to join and serve in the Second World War, of whom 36 paid the ultimate price. Once again Captain Ghulam Mohammad Malik assisted with recruiting volunteers. He died in January 1947 at the age of 88.

Dulmial is known in Pakistan as the 'Village with the Gun'. The story of this remarkable support for the British Army was not well known until a doctor from Nottingham, Dr Irfan Malik, began to research the history of his family. Two of his great-grandfathers fought in the First World War and two grandfathers took part in the Burma Campaign in the Second World War. Irfan Malik was born in Britain after his parents

Below, left: The 19th-century cannon in its final resting place in the village of Dulmial.

Below, centre: Captain Ghulam Mohammad Malik, Dulmial's most decorated officer.

Below, right: The Memorial in the village of Dulmial.

Opposite: The official unveiling ceremony of the Dulmial Gun in 1925.

Above: An advertisement for the Haig Fund published in 1946.

Right: 100 branches of the Legion were represented at a service in 1949 to mark the 21st anniversary of the death of Earl Haig.

emigrated there in the early 1960s. Although he was aware of Dulmial's history and the presence of the gun, he had no idea of the strong link it had to the British military.

'When I was growing up, I felt that Remembrance had little to do with me.' He explained, 'Then I learned the facts and the proud history of our village and I felt it important to share this with the world and to celebrate the relevance of Remembrance to my community in Britain and abroad. This is just a small part of our strong shared history.' Dr Malik's story was highlighted by the Legion on the centenary of the end of the First World War.

POST-SECOND WORLD WAR AND BEYOND

The Legion continued to keep faith with the Armed Forces community, working year in, year out, often quietly and unnoticed by the public, to help those in need of support. The Second World War generation had many of the same welfare needs as their First World War comrades and the Legion continued to fine-tune the help it offered through its branches. Any ex-Serviceman or woman can apply to the Legion for help and does not have to be a member. In the 1970s, when unemployment was high, there was increased call on welfare, but it was the ageing population that continued to be the main concern for the Legion.

In 1970 a branch chairman wrote of the 'hardening arteries in the villages', referring to the Legion branches whose members were ageing. 'This image is not calculated to appeal to the mass of the population … Age is the very devil, but it is a good deal easier to combat in a British Legion branch than in oneself provided the door is opened as wide as possible

to admit those younger men who do remain in the village.' He suggested that 'a Legion of all ages in co-operation might demonstrate to the rest of the country that the vast majority of modern youth are not drug-soaked drop-outs nor screaming revolutionaries as the Press would have us believe, but that they have at least as much idealism as any of their predecessors and are much less afraid of expressing it'. This call to a younger membership was only partially successful as the public had lost interest in the two world wars and was more concerned with demonstrating against current conflicts.

The Legion's fortunes waxed and waned with the vicissitudes of the second half of the 20th century, hitting a low point in the 1960s and 1970s when Britain was undergoing social and economic upheaval. There was IRA terrorism in Northern Ireland and on mainland

Britain. Army numbers in Northern Ireland doubled to 15,000 in the early 1970s. Scores of soldiers were shot and killed by snipers or saw their friends killed and suffered the pain of watching bands of locals cheering when the British dead were cleared away.[1] Many of the soldiers were in their late teens or early twenties from tough backgrounds in the estates of Britain's industrial cities. They sought revenge for this and carried out acts of criminal damage against the nationalists. By the end of 1971, the British Army was seen as a hostile occupying force, a tool of Unionist oppression.

That year the Legion celebrated its 50th birthday and was given the honour of a royal title, becoming the Royal British Legion. In a moment of understandable pride, the July 1971 *Journal* blew the Legion's trumpet:

Let us throw modesty aside and assert, without fear of contradiction, that the British Legion has made a deep and everlasting impression upon the social services of this country such as few other organisations have achieved. We can rightly claim to have altered the whole attitude of this country towards those who have served it in the armed forces, and by our campaigning, especially on behalf of the war disabled, to have brought benefits to whole sections of the community, outside our own ambit.

It was right to celebrate its achievements, but there was still much to do and the question of the Legion's place in the society at the time was unresolved. The Armed Forces were unpopular with the public at the height of the protests against the Vietnam War and the Legion was focused inwards on its ageing

Below, left: Peace protesters in Northern Ireland, 1976.

Below, right: First day cover for the 50th anniversary of the British Legion, 1971.

infrastructure and population, its concern over falling Poppy Appeal revenues and a shortfall of 50,000 collectors. All of this changed in 1982 when Prime Minister Margaret Thatcher sent a task force to the South Atlantic to defend the Falkland Islands. The war lasted for only ten weeks but its impact on the country was significant. It was the first war for a generation who had grown up with the Troubles in Northern Ireland as a sullen backdrop to the dark days of the 1970s and it had the effect of helping to restore the Armed Forces in the nation's eyes. That affected the Legion and by the turn of the century it was once again favourably in the public eye.

BECOMING A MODEL CHARITY

At the turn of the 21st century, as the Legion was about to mark its 80th anniversary, it carried out a major review called *Taking the Legion Forward*. The aim was to conduct a survey of the membership to see how it could be redefined to attract new and younger members. The survey showed that almost 50 per cent of the membership at the time was over the age of 70. It also had to ensure the charity was fit for purpose for the new century and conformed to the requirements of the Charity Commission. As the UK's leading ex-Service charity and one of the largest of the benevolent charities, it was important the Legion was seen to be moving forward in line with legislation and best practice. New regulations introduced by the Charities Act of 2006 meant that it had to make certain that its trustees had the skills, knowledge and experience to run the charity and that the membership and trustee functions were clearly separated. This resulted in a new make-up of the Board of Trustees

the heart of this change and he witnessed first-hand the move to the new building and simultaneously to the new form of governance. 'Change is always difficult and the move to Borough High Street was traumatic. The director general had to make big changes to bring the Legion into compliance with the Third Sector and that meant a new board with appointed trustees as well as ones elected from the membership.'

A NEW KID ON THE BLOCK

Help for Heroes came into being in 2007 in response to the Service personnel severely wounded in Iraq. Its launch caught the public mood and it was instantly successful as a laser-focused, nimble charity that had the single goal of improving the treatment and long-term care for these men and women. The Legion was caught on the back foot and admits that there were initially tensions as Help for Heroes entered the arena previously almost wholly occupied by the Legion. After a period of introspection and some anxieties, the Legion and Help for Heroes have come to a good understanding of what each can offer in terms of expertise in their area.

Today much of the Legion's work is subject to regulation, a result of increased health and safety issues, personal privacy and Charity Commission rules. It is something that frustrates older members, but it is important for the smooth running of the charity and the prosecution of its work. Falzon, who left the Legion and became a member of his local branch, an elected trustee on the board in 2014 and National Vice Chairman in 2019, has watched the change over the last decade and concluded: 'We are a totally different organisation to that which we were in 2011 and I believe we are going in the right direction.'

which had hitherto comprised elected women and men from the membership. The requirement now was for appointed trustees with expertise in finance, legal matters or property and the make-up of the board would be 6 appointed trustees, 12 elected trustees and one representative from the Women's Section. The membership, who had been involved in fundraising, welfare and Remembrance, felt this was a blow and it took time for the changes that were necessary to fulfil regulatory requirements to be accepted.

A separate board, the Membership Council, was set up to deal with membership issues, which in itself freed the Board of Trustees to focus on the question of governance and finance. A move of its headquarters within London from Pall Mall to Haig House on Borough High Street, Southwark, in 2009 marked a further change in the Legion's approach to areas of responsibility from fundraising and campaigning to welfare and Remembrance. Retired Lieutenant Colonel Joe Falzon, who worked at the Legion from 2001 to 2011, was at

Chapter 2

THE APPEAL OF THE POPPY

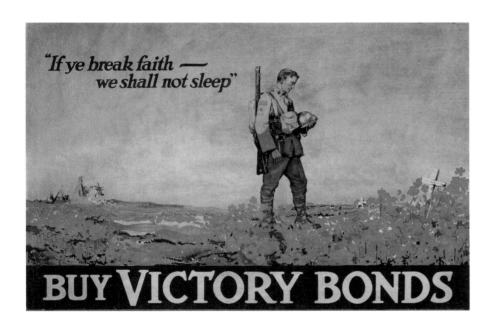

"If ye break faith —
we shall not sleep"

BUY VICTORY BONDS

Above: A Canadian
poster quoting lines from
John McCrae's poem,
'In Flanders Fields'.

On a bright sunny day in early September 1921, a sprightly 43-year-old French woman presented herself at the door of 26 Eccleston Square, the Legion's headquarters in Pimlico, London. She had an appointment to meet the General Secretary, Colonel Edward Heath, and the subject of the meeting was the poppy. She had been promoting the poppy as a symbol of Remembrance in the United States since the end of the First World War and it was her desire to spread the idea across the seas to Britain and the Empire. Her role in the story of the poppy is not well known. She was barely mentioned in the British press at the time and in subsequent history books she gets a line or two at most. Yet she is probably the single most important person in the story of the Remembrance Day poppy. Her name is Anna Guérin.

The inspiration behind the idea of the poppy as a symbol of Remembrance was a poem by the Canadian physician Major John McCrae. 'We shall not sleep', which became known as 'In Flanders Fields', was written in May 1915 and published anonymously in *Punch* that December. Sadly, John McCrae died of pneumonia in January 1918 and never lived to see his poem become the inspiration for worldwide Remembrance of those who die in war.

Above: 1921 illustrated cover for McCrae's poem, 'In Flanders Fields'.

Left: Major John McCrae, c.1917.

The first record of a Poppy Day in Britain was during the First World War, four months before McCrae's poem was published. On 21 August 1915 an appeal, using the poppy as it symbol, was held in South Shields in aid of the Ingham Infirmary and local Poor Children's Association. The appeal raised almost £200 (£20,700). This was followed by several other Poppy Days over the course of the war, but they were small scale and limited to individual towns.

The person who claimed to be the originator of the poppy as a national symbol of Remembrance was an American academic and writer, Moina Michael. She was so inspired by McCrae's poem that she wrote her own verse, 'We shall keep the faith', in response and vowed she would always wear a red poppy as a symbol of Remembrance. After the war she taught a class for disabled Servicemen and saw their need for financial and occupational support. It was then that she convinced the American Legion Auxiliary to adopt the poppy as its symbol in 1921. In her autobiography, *The Miracle Flower*, Moina Michael claimed responsibility for the worldwide adoption of the poppy, effectively writing Madame Guérin out of the story.[2]

At the same time, Madame Guérin was lecturing in the United States, raising money for her charity and simultaneously promoting the idea of the poppy as the symbol of Remembrance. While Moina Michael remained focused on the United States, Madame Guérin had wider ambitions. By the end of 1920 she had been responsible for Poppy Days in several US states and in 1921 she turned her attention to Canada. In June she was to be found in Toronto addressing a meeting of the Catholic Women's League of Canada. The *Toronto Daily Star* reported how she had made a 'touching appeal on behalf of the children and women of the war

JEANNE d'ARC filant   Mme Guérin

Madame Anna Guérin was no stranger to Britain. She had lived and worked throughout the British Isles as a lecturer for the Alliance Française in the early years of the 20th century. Born in Vallon in the Ardèche in 1878, Anna Alix Boulle had an unusual career. She married young and went with her husband to Madagascar where she ran a school. She was a passionate teacher and an outstanding communicator, creating for herself a role of significance in the capital Tananarive (now Antananarivo). Her first marriage ended in divorce in 1907 and she married Eugène Guérin three years later. In 1911 her husband left for Sudan and Anna came to Britain with her two daughters by her first marriage. She worked as an 'artistic lecturer', which, when unpacked, meant that she performed to audiences in costume and speaking French with a translator. She spoke about Madagascar, but she also talked about prominent women from France's history, appearing variously as Marie Antoinette, Joséphine Bonaparte and Joan of Arc (left). She was described as the Sarah Bernhardt of the lecture platform, in reference to the famous French actress of the day.

When the First World War broke out Madame Guérin went to the United States where she immediately began fundraising for those made destitute by war. She sent the proceeds of her lectures to the Secours de France in Paris and once the United States entered the war, in 1917, she was able to describe herself as a war lecturer. After the Armistice she returned briefly to France to help set up La Ligue des enfants de France et d'Amérique (the league for the protection of children in France and America). Back in the United States she returned to her energetic fundraising but she also began to promote the idea of the poppy being adopted as the symbol of Remembrance. She was not the first person to the party, but she was most certainly the energy behind what became the concept of Poppy Day in Britain and the Commonwealth. An original French cotton poppy (1921) is pictured below.

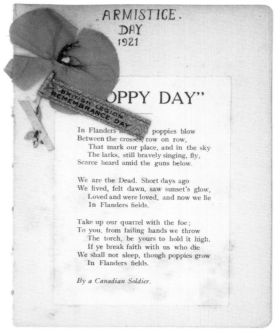

ARMISTICE.
DAY
1921

"POPPY DAY"

In Flanders ~~~~ poppies blow
Between the crosses, row on row,
    That mark our place, and in the sky
    The larks, still bravely singing, fly,
Scarce heard amid the guns below.

We are the Dead. Short days ago
We lived, felt dawn, saw sunset's glow,
    Loved and were loved, and now we lie
    In Flanders fields.

Take up our quarrel with the foe:
To you, from failing hands we throw
    The torch, be yours to hold it high.
    If ye break faith with us who die
We shall not sleep, though poppies grow
    In Flanders fields.

By a Canadian Soldier.

Above, left: Early use of a poppy as a symbol of Remembrance, 1917.

Above, right: An original French silk poppy from 1921.

devastated areas in France, urging the wearing of a red poppy on armistice memorial day in memory "of your boys and our boys who sleep side by side in Flanders field".'

It was not difficult to convince the Canadian veterans' organisations, who were proud of their association with John McCrae, and Madame Guérin was able to leave for Britain in late August having achieved her aim. By the time she arrived in Liverpool and set forth for London, Madame Guérin was not only convinced that she could persuade the fledgling British Legion to accept her idea but she also knew she could help it to organise the

appeal nationwide. Her experience of fundraising and working with women's groups had convinced her of the value of using women as volunteers to create a network of distribution and collection.

Before leaving for Britain she told the Canadians that she was hoping to ask the Prince of Wales to become head of the Poppy Day movement in Britain. Whether this was wishful thinking or whether she had actually made contact with the Palace is not recorded but it is the case that when she approached Colonel Crosfield, the Legion's Vice Chairman, she believed she was pushing at an open door.

She wrote of the meeting in her brief memoir:

Field Marshall Haig, the President, called a meeting where I explain the Idea which was adopted immediately, but they had no money in the Treasury to order their Poppies. It was September and the Armistice day in November. I offered them to order their Poppies in France for them, so my own responsibility, that they would pay them after. Gladly they accepted my offer.[3]

Not everyone was as enthusiastic as Madame Guérin suggested. General Secretary Colonel Heath's version of events differs from hers. He recalled how Colonel Crosfield had asked him to meet 'a Madame Guérin' who arrived with a small number of artificial poppies made by French women for sale to raise money for children in the devastated areas of France. She asked him whether the Legion would be interested in adopting the emblem as a means of raising money. She explained that there were two firms in France ready to supply poppies to Britain. He put the idea to the Finance Committee, which was concerned with raising funds for benevolence. The reaction, he recalled, was swift: 'Poppies! Who wants poppies? Madame Guérin – who is she? What are her credentials? Do the two French firms exist?'

Despite the scepticism of members of the Finance Committee, the Legion decided to send a representative, Sir Herbert Brown, to Paris to investigate. He returned with the news that Madame Guérin was genuine and the firms stood ready to make poppies for the Legion. The Finance Committee took up Madame Guérin's offer of funding the manufacture of a million poppies on the condition they would be paid for after Poppy Day, with a small contribution from the British appeal for her charity in France.

On 6 October Earl Haig announced that he wished 11 November 1921 to be known as Remembrance Day and that it would be a 'Poppy Day'. The Legion decided to have additional poppies manufactured in Britain and commissioned eight million. The organisation of the sale and distribution of nine million poppies was an immense task. Nevertheless, the Legion was determined it would succeed and they appointed a highly able former officer, Captain W G Willcox, to be in charge. He had just eight weeks to organise the entire Appeal from scratch.

Madame Guérin was back in France ensuring that the poppies were made and delivered to the Legion in good time. Those poppies were simple, bright-red pieces of fabric with a green stalk and a little banner that read on one side 'British Legion Remembrance Day' and on the other 'Made by the Women and Children. The devastated areas of France.' Earl Haig's poppy, which was made in Britain, had five petals, black stitching in the middle with little beads and a leaf. This is now in the collection of Poppyscotland.

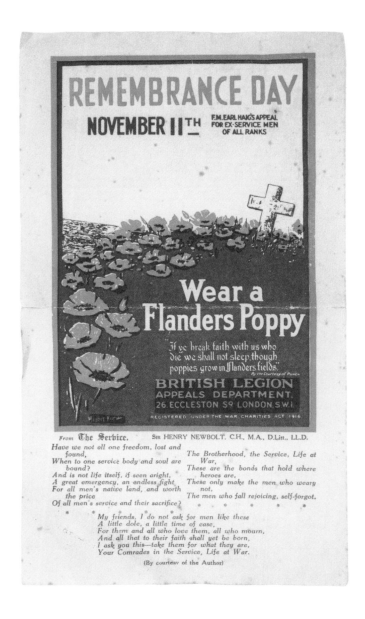

British newspapers ran promotional articles about the plans for Poppy Day, using lines from 'In Flanders Fields', but made no mention of the energetic Madame Guérin. It is unclear whether this was deliberate or whether the 'Haig Fund' that was created was of such overwhelming importance to the British public that her name was not heard. One way or another Anna Guérin has disappeared from the history of the poppy in Britain with only the odd mention here and there. Yet she continued to champion her cause and New Zealand bought its poppies from France until 1928, when it switched to the Poppy Factory in Britain.

There could be no doubt that the idea of adopting the poppy as Britain's symbol of Remembrance was an immediate success. When the nine million poppies ran out, people improvised with other flowers. The press was delighted and devoted many column inches to the Poppy Day Appeal. *The Times* noted that the work of selling poppies had largely been undertaken by women, many from the Women's Section, but also others unaffiliated to the Legion, who were keen to lend their support to the cause.

Above, left to right: Poppy with forget-me-nots, 1922; silk poppy, 1923–4; crepe-paper poppy, 1926.

Right to far right: Early poppy pins from the 1920s, including back and front of a cardboard poppy for children.

Above, left to right: Cotton
poppy; 'lawn' fabric poppy;
poppy, 1930s.

Right to far right: Poppy
with sateen front, 1930s;
poppy, 1939.

THE LATE EARL HAIG AT BRITISH LEGION POPPY FACTORY. 26173.

Above: Earl Haig was a regular visitor to the Poppy Factory in Richmond up to his death in January 1928.

Not only had Poppy Day entered the public's imagination as a good way to mark Remembrance, but it had also proven a financial success for the Legion. By the end of 1921 the Appeals Committee reported a figure of £106,000 (£5.2 million) in takings. The cost of the poppies had been almost a fifth of that amount and the Legion had to decide whether it could manufacture the poppies exclusively in Britain for a smaller outlay.

The decision to do so introduced one of the most popular of all the Legion's projects. The Poppy Factory was founded in the Old Kent Road by Major George Howson, who had earlier launched the Disabled Society for the improvement of artificial limbs, and Major Brunel Cohen. Howson had been one of several applicants to the Legion, who had advertised for a hospital or institution that would be prepared to give the work of making poppies to as many disabled ex-Servicemen as possible. The Legion supported the setting up of the factory as a separate not-for-profit organisation, which employed wounded, injured and sick veterans. It ordered 30 million poppies for the 1922 Appeal and 41 disabled men employed that year successfully fulfilled the order.

The Prince of Wales made regular visits to see the work and to meet the men, many of whom had severe disabilities. From the start the atmosphere in the Poppy Factory was cheerful. The men took pride in their work and quickly developed the skills needed to manufacture poppies on a vast scale, making thousands each week, which were sent for storage in a warehouse at King's Cross.

By 1924 the factory had outgrown its premises and a move to Richmond followed, to a former brewery and later to a custom-built factory on the adjoining site. Major Howson expanded his workforce to 190

Below, left to right:
Poppy Factory workers
at Bermondsey cheer the
Legion's Patron, the Prince
of Wales, on a visit in
1924; the Prince inspects
an RAF wreath at the
Poppy Factory.

with a further 300 men on the waiting list to join when the opportunity arose. Accommodation was built for the men working at the factory and there was soon a community of families living around the site.

So quickly did the poppy take off as the national emblem of Remembrance after the 1921 Poppy Day Appeal that everyone wanted to be able to wear one, including the serving members of the Army, Navy and Royal Air Force. The King's Regulations had to be changed in 1923 to allow members of the Armed Forces to wear them on their uniform, a reminder of just how strictly rules over dress code were enforced. Over the course of the next decade Remembrance Day and the Poppy Day Appeal bedded in as part of the national life of Britain. The money raised from the appeal grew year on year, reaching the magical

half-million mark in 1928 when £503,348 (£32 million) was raised and this sum continued to rise, with the exception of 1932 at the height of the Great Depression, to £527,302 in 1935. This total meant the Legion had raised almost £6 million (£385 million) in 15 years and Poppyscotland almost £1 million (£64 million).

The design for the red poppy had been unified by 1922 with a black button in the middle with HF (Haig Fund) stamped on it. There were four designs to suit all pockets. The most expensive, at 1 shilling (£2.50), was a large poppy made from silk. A smaller silk poppy sold for 6d (£1.25) and a cheaper one made from lawn or cotton cost 3d (62p). A cardboard poppy for children sold for 2d (40p). A Poppy Motor Mascot was introduced in 1930 and proved popular with car owners. That year the

EDWARD, PRINCE OF WALES

It was stated in the Legion's *Journal* of 1935 that, 'No royal King or Prince in history has ever been so intimately associated with the rank and file of the fighting forces of the Crown as was King Edward as Prince of Wales.' He was loved by the Legion's membership because of his bravery in the war. Although a sailor by training and heir to the British crown by destiny, he resolved to be part of the action on the Western Front.

One officer charged with keeping him safe wrote: 'It was useless. After a time, HRH insisted upon going into the trenches whenever he wished. It was helpless to confine his ADC duties to zones of comparative safety. My hair turned grey with the continued anxiety.' The Prince's presence was an inspiration to the fighting troops and the fact that he was enduring the same grim conditions as they were proved a military asset of immense value. Officers and men up and down the line knew of his determination not to spare himself. One man was heard to say: 'We would go to hell itself for that boy.'

When he was approached to become Patron of the fledgling Legion in 1921, Edward, Prince of Wales could not have been a more popular choice. And he did not disappoint the membership. He was a regular visitor to the Poppy Factory, Preston Hall and other centres of Legion activity and attended the annual conference at the Queen's Hall as often as he could. He made frequent tours around the country and was always received with rapturous cheers and usually a Legion Guard of Honour. He was known for his interest in the welfare of the ex-Servicemen and he led by example, donating £150,000 (£7.3 million) to the Unity Relief Fund to help out-of-work ex-Servicemen. He attended almost every Festival of Remembrance at the Royal Albert Hall and took part in the Great Pilgrimage to France and Belgium in 1928.

In the photographs the Prince is shown laying a wreath at the Cenotaph in 1923 and talking to Sepoy Subadar Ishar Singh VC at Richmond in 1929.

Upon his abdication Edward VIII, former Prince of Wales and Patron of the Legion for 15 years, was exiled to France and demoted to the Duke of Windsor. His place as Patron was taken by the next in line to the throne, the Duke of York, who was crowned King George VI on 12 May 1937. When he died in 1952 Her Majesty The Queen took over the role of Patron of the Legion, a title she still holds.

amount of money raised from the Poppy Day Appeal
had risen to £524,000 (£34.5 million) and accounted for
96 per cent of the Legion's income. Today the Appeal
raises more than £54 million annually and constitutes
approximately a third of the Legion's income.

Poppy-making remains a year-round business, with
the two months before Remembrance Sunday being
the busiest when it comes to the distribution of the
millions of poppies across the world. Today there
are two factories. The original factory in Richmond
continues to make 4.5 million poppies a year plus
wreaths and the crepe-paper poppy petals for the
Festival of Remembrance, which are lighter than the
regular poppies and therefore float down slowly. It also
makes related products, such as the wooden poppy

stakes adorned with the Christian cross, the Muslim
crescent, the Hindu *Om*, the Star of David and the
Celtic cross. The factory in Aylesford, Kent, which acts
as a warehouse for all poppies, wreaths and other
memorabilia, has four poppy machines that produce
31.5 million poppies annually. The four components of
the poppy are the red petals and green leaves, which
are made from paper, and the black central button and
the green stem which are plastic and are made by
inmates at HM Prison Lewes. Today there are scores
of different designs of poppy memorabilia with buttons,
pins, flags, windmills, T-shirts and even collars for dogs.
Yet the basic design of the poppy remains so simple
and iconic that any change from the design seems
unthinkable. Or does it?

Above, left: The Poppy Factory diversified in the 1930s and made Christmas crackers for a few years.

Above, right: Over the years the Poppy Factory developed automated systems but the need for a substantial workforce remained and the factory continued to employ men disabled by their war service.

Opposite: Men are seen here placing wires in the bitumen centres for poppies, c.1950s.

Opposite, left; Remembrance Day poster from 1923.

Opposite, right: Lithographic advertisement issued by E Sharp & Sons in 1942.

Right: Front cover of the *Journal* from October 1956.

Opposite, top left: An elephant joins the Poppy Day Appeal in Leeds, 1924.

Opposite, top right: Betty Leleu collecting in London, c.1927.

Opposite, below left to right: Collectors in Dorking; ex-Serviceman at the Field of Remembrance.

Above and right: From the earliest days the Poppy Collectors have been a feature of Remembrancetide, whether wives, widows or daughters, ex-Servicemen or veterans disabled by war.

Top, right: Collectors leaving for England, April 1958.

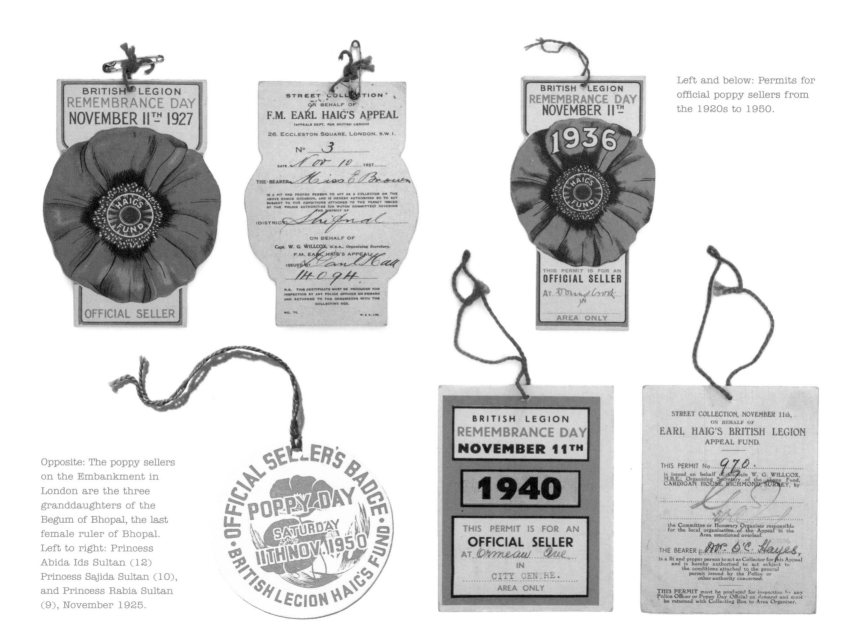

Opposite: The poppy sellers on the Embankment in London are the three granddaughters of the Begum of Bhopal, the last female ruler of Bhopal. Left to right: Princess Abida Ids Sultan (12) Princess Sajida Sultan (10), and Princess Rabia Sultan (9), November 1925.

Left and below: Permits for official poppy sellers from the 1920s to 1950.

Opposite, top left to right: A rare example of a collecting tin from 1921; old tin with 1983 label; mid-1920s tin.

Opposite, bottom left to right: The war chest appeared in 1940; the lion in the 1990s.

Left and below: A collection of tins from the 1970s (left) to 2020 (bottom right).

THE PAPER POPPY

The switch from silk and cotton to paper poppies in the early 1970s was made for sound commercial reasons but it turned out to be a disaster on a wet Remembrance Sunday in 1978 when the cotton-based red poppies bled onto the white uniforms of the Royal Marines Band. As a result, the Legion sought a new paper supplier that could produce dye-fast red and green paper to be supplied to the factories in November each year.

A shout went out to paper mills for assistance in finding a bleed-free paper that could be produced quickly and in large quantities. The contract went to James Cropper Plc at Burnside Mills near Kendal, a company that had been making paper on the site since 1845. Today it produces paper for high-end brands such as Louis Vuitton and Smythson, as well as for the Legion. Cropper delivers 3 miles (5km) of paper to the Legion's two poppy factories every year, the red paper being on 1,500-metre rolls and the green on 1,000, reflecting the balance of red and green in the made-up poppies.

There have been questions over the years about the significance of the colours in the poppy. Does the red of the petals refer to the blood spilled on the battlefields of France and Flanders? No, it is red because poppies have red petals. Does the green represent the trees that grew on those fields, or the grass that surrounds the graves? No, it is green because poppy leaves are green. And the black button? It is black because the centre of a poppy is black. Today's simplified poppy design is ideal for mass production by machine. In the interwar years, when the poppies were made mainly by hand, the design was closer to the flower itself, with a blousy

shaped head and little white seeds around the black central button. The wreaths were rich with spiky green foliage and lush red poppies.

In 1934 white poppies appeared alongside the Legion's red ones. These were sold by members of the Co-operative Women's Guild, which had been formed a year earlier, and were designed, they announced, to represent 'the sacred cause of Justice and the freedom of the world' – words inscribed on the Grave of the Unknown Warrior in Westminster Abbey. This was confusing as it was precisely the reason why the Servicemen had laid down their lives in the war. The following year the Peace Pledge Union also adopted the white poppy, accusing the Legion of glorifying war in

some way with the use of the Flanders poppy. It was a sad misinterpretation of what the Legion stood for.

The white poppy was forgotten during the Second World War, when the country stood shoulder to shoulder against a common enemy, but it made a reappearance in the late 1960s. This time it had a wider political significance as anti-war sentiment in Britain ran high. At the same time, the British Armed Forces were unpopular with the public. Legion members were unhappy about the white poppy, especially those who had recently been in Northern Ireland during the Troubles. Today the Legion takes a more relaxed view of different-coloured poppies, including rainbow poppies to reflect the LGBTQ+ community. However, the

Legion's own poppy offering is always red. The reaction of the public towards the red Remembrance Poppy over the years is a mark of the societal changes and mood swings in the country in the last 100 years.

Money came not just from the sale of poppies in the UK but also from Poppy Day Appeals worldwide. In 1934 the *Journal* reported that no fewer than 51 countries regularly held Poppy Days. Cities including Kabul in Afghanistan, Damascus in Syria, Managua in Nicaragua and San Salvador in El Salvador all sent takings to London, which were then distributed nationally and internationally. That was in addition to the countries that manufactured their own poppies using the local ex-Service associations. Where that was not possible, overseas branches could order their poppies from Richmond. The consignments destined for remote areas of the globe would leave the Poppy Factory as early as April. Most of the shipping companies carried poppies free of charge and port authorities waived fees and taxes. Some of the most isolated outposts were so remote it took weeks from the ports to the final place of sale. British sheep farmers in South America received their consignment by mule cart which had travelled hundreds of miles into the interior.

The size of the Poppy Factory workforce grew year on year. By 1928 when Major Howson had taken on responsibility for the supply of poppies for New Zealand, the number of men working in Richmond stood at 270. The numbers went up again in 1935 and by the outbreak of the Second World War stood at 365, of which more than three-quarters were classed as severely disabled. With wives and children, this community numbered over 1,000 people. In the decades that followed, the Poppy Factory continued to build a supportive environment for veterans with physical and mental

health conditions, developing a strong understanding of the complex challenges that many face. Today, the charity's support reaches far beyond the factory into communities across England, Wales and Northern Ireland, helping ex-Forces men and women on their journey into all kinds of employment.

The Poppy Factory's employability service launched in 2010 and now makes up 90 per cent of its work. Each year it helps hundreds of veterans with a mental or physical health condition to thrive in the workplace, wherever they are based.

Opposite: The Poppy Factory at Richmond has been on the present site since 1926.

Below, left to right: Poppy production at Richmond is partly automated but many processes, such as the Remembrance stakes (below right) have to be completed by hand.

Overleaf: Poppy production at Richmond, 2020.

WE ARE THE LEGION

Poppy production and
packing at Aylesford,
autumn 2020.

What would happen to the British Legion in the Second World War? That was the question on everyone's lips in the Legion's headquarters at 26 Eccleston Square in the summer of 1939. Would there be a Poppy Day at all in November? The government's Committee of Civil Defence considered aerial warfare as the most dangerous unknown in any future conflict. Based on the experience of air raids at the end of the First World War, the committee estimated that the likely number of casualties per ton of bombs dropped would be 50, with two-thirds injured and one-third killed outright. As they anxiously watched the build-up of Hermann Goering's Luftwaffe, the fear of a *kolossal* (massive) German attack grew.

In the event those bombs did not fall and many of the three million people who had been evacuated at the end of August and beginning of September returned to the large cities, causing chaos for the authorities. By November the country had settled down into the strange period known as the Phoney War and Remembrance Day was held as usual. That year, to the Legion's surprise, the takings were up. Even at the height of the Blitz the following year the Appeal rose and through the subsequent years until November 1945, when the Poppy Appeal hit £1 million (£43 million).

As a result of wartime shortages, the poppies appeared in just two designs. This was simplified after the war to a single design, a simple red poppy with the black HF button, reflecting the state of austerity Britain of the late 1940s. The green leaf was reintroduced in 1975.

Left: This 1942 poppy reflects the shortage of materials and austerity caused by rationing.

Above: A waxed car poppy, 1945.

Opposite, top left to right: Poppy spray, 1950s; poppy with leaf, 1958.

Opposite, below left to right: Double sateen poppy, 1950s; poppy, 1950s; poppy, 1987.

In 2010 Simon Cowell wore a crocheted poppy
emblem by jewellery designer Kleshna on his lapel
while judging *The X Factor*. It immediately caught on.
Enamel and crystal poppies were worn by presenters
of the daytime television show *Loose Women*, and
by the pop band The Saturdays. Although there was
criticism from some who were opposed to 'blinged-up'
poppies, the Legion was delighted. 'Shows like *The
X Factor* and *Strictly Come Dancing* are watched by
millions of viewers. It is bound to raise awareness and
encourage people to wear a poppy', said a spokesman
in 2011. Profits from the sale of poppy bling adds a
large boost to the annual Poppy Appeal and the offering
from the Poppy Shop is designed to suit all wallets.

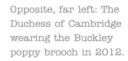

Opposite, far left: The Duchess of Cambridge wearing the Buckley poppy brooch in 2012.

From opposite, top left to right: Codebreakers Brooch; Second World War Armed Forces pin; pewter round poppy pin; heart of poppies.

From opposite, below left to right: Piece by Piece brooch; soutache poppy lapel pin; crystal flower brooch; poppy pearl and crystal wreath; Remember Together lapel pin.

Above: Poppy Popsy at
the Annual Conference,
Birmingham, 1980.

Opposite, left: A poppy taxi
on the 50th anniversary of
the Legion, 1971.

POPPY POPSIES

One of the features of the early Poppy Day Appeals
were the collectors. They were predominantly women,
often widows or daughters of men who had been killed
or injured in the war. The organisation of the Appeal was
a colossal effort run by Captain Willcox in London and
spread out across the branch network and communities
around the country. Some leaders of the volunteer army
of collectors were members of the Women's Section,
others were not, but all pulled together year after year
in whatever weather conditions prevailed in the lead
up to Remembrance Day. In the 1920s the spread
of ages reflected those affected by the war: young
widows, mothers, daughters, as well as wives of men
who returned safely. As the years went on this army
of female collectors aged and began to retire from the
arduous task of collecting money on the street or house
to house. By the 1970s there was a severe shortage
of people willing to do the collections. The Legion
estimated that 50,000 volunteers were required to plug
the gap and the pressure to find new volunteers grew.

The Legion experimented with new ways of
marketing its vital brand to attract younger people
to the Poppy Appeal. One of the more colourful, but
perhaps to today's taste questionable, methods was
the introduction of Miss British Legion. It sought to
emulate the public's fascination with the Miss World
pageant, which had its highest ratings in the 1970s and
1980s when it was watched by a television audience
of 27.5 million. It is not surprising that the Legion could
see merit in tapping into the enthusiasm for pretty
girls wearing alarmingly short skirts, selling poppies
or posing for pictures with notable members of the
Legion and other society figures. They became known

affectionately as the Poppy Popsies. Fortunately, that phase did not last more than a decade. The Popsies were phased out when a surge of enthusiasm for the Armed Forces after the successful conclusion of the Falklands War gave the Legion its largest Poppy Appeal taking in ten years.

The refocus on the military and the Legion's strong message about the needs of ex-Servicemen and women from all wars, not just the First and Second World Wars, had an impact. By the beginning of the 21st century the Legion's confidence had been restored and the public's regard for Remembrance and the Poppy Appeal had increased. Recently the annual appeal has marked major anniversaries such as D-Day 75, and the end of the Second World War in both Europe and the Far East in 2020 with VE Day 75 and VJ Day 75.

THE SPICE GIRLS

In 1997 the Legion engaged a PR team who launched a campaign to encourage more people to wear a poppy and to exceed the £16.2 million raised the previous year. In a brilliant move the team succeeded in getting the band of the moment, the Spice Girls, to appear pro bono alongside Vera Lynn. With a week to go to the Appeal the team used an exclusive in the *Sun* newspaper to announce the launch. Each of the major papers, TV and radio stations was invited to send one representative. The campaign cost £10,000 and the launch was covered on 17 national TV bulletins and 92 radio programmes. Not only did it achieve blanket coverage in the national press, but many papers carried the poppy on their mastheads and Channel 4's soap *Brookside* featured a tray of poppies in one of its episodes.

Daily Mirror columnist Tony Parsons commented: 'It was a shrewd move and very appropriate. Vera Lynn was the Spice Girl of her day.' For the record, the 1997 takings totalled £17,281,382.

Fundraising is a large part of the Legion's work and is as vital today as it was in the early years. The Poppy Appeal is the world's largest street cash collection and raises more than £50 million annually for the Legion's welfare programmes, representing a third of the Legion's income each year. It is carried out at branch and national level, with teams of collectors standing in wind, rain or sun for hours on end at markets, on street corners, in shops or at events. The street collections are what the public is most aware of; the City Poppy Days (held in London, Cardiff, Bristol, Leeds, Birmingham and Manchester, involving uniformed personnel from the Army, Navy and Royal Air Force, and veterans and their supporters) receive widespread media coverage.

Members of the Legion have a reputation for creative fundraising that can range from sponsored sporting events, hikes or cycle rides to activities such as a green initiative over the summer of 2020. Retired Commander Stafford Seward OBE, MBE, RN, Chairman of Kilmington Branch in Devon, replicated the fortnightly green waste collection service, which had been suspended during the coronavirus pandemic, by collecting the waste with a tractor and trailer. Rather than charging for the service he requested donations for the Poppy Appeal. Over a period of six weeks he and two helpers collected waste from every household in the village three times and raised £2,000 for the Legion.

Above: Advertisement on the back of a London Routemaster Bus, November 2012.

Opposite: Chelsea Pensioners, veterans and volunteers from the general public all play a crucial role in collecting for the Poppy Appeal – including Darcey Bussell (bottom right).

Despite the pandemic, the 2020 Poppy Appeal went ahead, albeit in a socially distanced form. Included in the appeal were (opposite) Barry and Tricia Oldham; (below, left to right) Samantha Rawlinson and Flyle Hussain with his wife; (bottom, left to right) Bill Taylor and Nicole Brown.

Below and opposite: *Blood Swept Lands and Seas of Red* by ceramic artist Paul Cummins and stage designer Tom Piper at the Tower of London, 2014.

Below, left: A traditional poppy stake is fixed to the railings by a visitor to the exhibition, 2014.

In 2014 the world marked the 100th anniversary of the beginning of the First World War. By that time, there were no veterans still alive in Britain; Harry Patch had died in 2009 at the venerable age of 111. Yet the commemorations were immense. A magnificent field of poppies entitled *Blood Swept Lands and Seas of Red* was created by artist Paul Cummins and stage designer Tom Piper at the Tower of London. A total of 888,246 handmade ceramic poppies, marking the number of British and Commonwealth military fatalities in the First World War, were 'planted' in the tower's moat and made to tumble down the walls from a window. It took over 21,000 volunteers four months to create the largest art installation ever seen at the Tower. The involvement of the Yeoman Warders, each of whom had served in one of the British Armed Forces, was of special significance.

The display captured the popular imagination and by the end of the exhibition more than five million people from all over the world had visited London to see the poppies. How delighted would Madame Anna Guérin have been to witness such an outpouring of emotion over the symbol that she brought to the attention of the British Legion in September 1921.

After the exhibition was over, individual poppies were sold to subscribers for £25 and the money divided between various military charities. The Legion was among the charities that benefited from a share of the £23 million raised from the sale. *Blood Swept Lands and Seas of Red* was so popular that it went on tour at venues in all four countries of the United Kingdom for the next four years.

With such a public endorsement of the poppy anew, the Legion was able to capitalise on the success and produce more and varied designs for consumption. However, it is the simple red poppy with its green leaf and black button that has the power to remind the country every November of the sacrifice of men and women who laid down their lives for our freedom.

THE KHADI POPPY

In a speech in the House of Lords on 5 November 2018, Jitesh Gadhia, Baron Gadhia of Northwood, expressed admiration for the remarkable courage and sacrifice of the 1.5 million men from undivided India who fought alongside the British in the First World War. He spoke of the arrival of Indian troops on the Western Front in September 1914 being critical to preventing a German breakthrough. In all, 74,000 Indians serving in multiple continents, from the Somme to the Sahara, never returned home.

A year earlier, Lord Gadhia had presented an initiative to the Royal British Legion to recognise the contribution made by India in both world wars. His ambition was to make 'Global Britain' a reality and not just a slogan. This would be represented by a poppy. It was difficult to choose a colour and there was concern it might dilute the message if it were not red. Then, in what he described as a 'light-bulb moment', he and his group overseeing the 2017 UK–India Year of Culture, realised the power would come from a red poppy, identical to the Legion poppy, but made out of khadi, the homespun cotton made famous by Mahatma Gandhi.

The symbolism of the khadi poppy is not just in the recognition of the outsized contribution of Indian soldiers but in invoking Gandhi's own courage and solidarity. 'In keeping with that spirit, the design is identical in almost every respect, including its colour, to the traditional poppy, apart from the hugely symbolic twist of using khadi. It does not seek to single out just one group but remembers everyone: it is a unifying symbol for us all.'

Lord Gadhia concluded: 'I hope that it also sends a powerful signal to Asians growing up in Britain and inspires the next generation to understand their own identity. They should know that their parents and grandparents did not just come here as immigrants. Our ancestors fought for this country and for freedom and democracy, even though they lived in a colony at the time. We therefore have as great a stake here as anyone else. Indeed, everyone from the Commonwealth should be proud of the role which their forebears played in shaping the destiny of the world a century ago.'

Opposite: The khadi poppy.

Above, left: Virat Kohli and Joe Root launching the khadi poppy at Lords, 2018.

Above, right: The khadi poppy was distributed at 'Diwali on Trafalgar Square', October 2018.

REMEMBRANCE

Chapter 3

————————————————

REMEMBRANCE

————————————————

REMEMBRANCE

The history of Remembrance is a long and evolving one. In the distant past, when wars were fought in faraway lands with a small professional army, the men who were the backbone of the Army and the Royal Navy were nameless. If you look at any military memorial from the years before the 20th century you will see monuments to generals and admirals, Field Marshals and Commanders, but of the ordinary soldier or sailor you will see little or no mention. It was only with the South African Wars at the turn at the 20th century that people began to list the names of men on memorials.

The First World War changed everything. For one, the deaths from an industrialised war were on such an unimaginable scale that almost every household in Britain was affected by the loss of a close family member or a friend in the community. Only 53 civil parishes in England and Wales were designated Thankful Villages, meaning that all their sons and daughters returned home. No villages in Scotland or on the island of Ireland escaped without loss. For another, much of the fighting was taking place just the other side of the Channel and families were desperate to see the final resting place of their loved ones. But finally, it was the fact that the war had swallowed up millions of volunteers, and later conscripted men, who became fodder for the hungry beast of war. Families lost one,

two, in some cases more of their young men and for each man killed there was the tragedy of a family's loss, a sweetheart's bereavement, a widow's agony or the children's sadness at never seeing their father again.

As the death figures grew, there was a clamour from relatives to know where their men were buried. An informal scheme began whereby graves were located and photographed. The name of the deceased, if known, was written on the wooden cross. At first this was done in pencil but later in pen, to ensure permanence until after the war was over. The photographs and details were sent to the Red Cross and the information was then relayed to the families. This was put onto a more formal footing in 1915 when Fabian Ware, a volunteer ambulance driver, sought permission to acquire land from the French, usually adjoining existing cemeteries, for more formal burial. The French government offered land to the British for free and in perpetuity. Over the course of the war this work grew as the number of dead rose and the names of battles became synonymous with major losses: the Somme, Ypres, Passchendaele, and further afield,

Sir Edwin Lutyens was one of Britain's pre-eminent architects at the turn of the 20th century. In 1917 he was approached by the newly formed Imperial War Graves Commission to advise on the design for its cemeteries in France and Belgium and, later, on the memorials to the missing. Lutyens felt strongly that the architectural form should be abstract and reflect a humanist rather than Anglican approach so as to ensure the cemeteries and memorials would be acceptable to men and women of all faiths and none. He described his Stone of Remembrance, which is to be found in any cemetery with more than 1,000 burials, as 'one great fair stone of fine proportions, twelve feet in length, lying raised upon three steps, of which the first and third shall be twice the width of the second'.

In 1919 Lutyens was asked by Prime Minister David Lloyd George to design a temporary 'catafalque' or coffin stand for the Victory Parade to be held in London that July. Apparently completing the design in just one day, he produced the idea not for a catafalque but for a cenotaph or 'empty tomb'. Although it appears simple, the final, stone version is a monument of great subtlety, 'all its surfaces being curved according to calculations based on the entasis or optical corrections of the Parthenon'.[4]

The Cenotaph (pictured right) was unveiled in 1920 and is at the heart of Remembrance every November. There is a replica of the Cenotaph in Hong Kong which was unveiled in 1923, and others in a few cities in the UK including Southampton (top right).

Gallipoli and Kut. The Imperial War Graves Commission, now the Commonwealth War Graves Commission (CWGC), came into being in May 1917 and today cares for the memories in its cemeteries and on its memorials of 1.7 million men and women who died in the two world wars. Like the Legion it honours the dead with equality, regardless of race, rank or religion.

The CWGC and the Royal British Legion have no formal partnership, but they work closely together, especially during commemorations and pilgrimages. Visits to battlefields and war cemeteries began soon after the end of the First World War and have continued for more than a century.

Right: 'What memories are crowded here! Eleven o'clock in Whitehall – the moving spectacle that fitly focussed the Empire's tribute of Remembrance.'

Far right: 1920s postcard showing the 'Ole Bill' bus at the permanent Cenotaph.

THE NATIONAL SERVICE OF REMEMBRANCE

If the poppy is the symbol of Remembrance, the heart of the Service of Remembrance itself is the Cenotaph in Whitehall in the centre of London. Created by Sir Edwin Lutyens in 1919 as a temporary wood-and-plaster structure erected for a peace parade after the end of the First World War, it struck a chord with the public. As the repatriation of remains had been forbidden during the war, families had no graves to tend in their hometowns and villages, so the Cenotaph quickly came to represent a tomb for all those lost abroad. More than a million people visited the Cenotaph in the week after the Victory Parade to lay flowers at its foot and pay their respects to the dead.

Within days there were clamours in the press and in letters to the government for the Cenotaph to be made a permanent feature in Whitehall. The government bowed to pressure. Ten days after the Victory Parade it announced that there would be a permanent memorial in Whitehall. Lutyens made minor alterations to the design that would work better in stone than in wood.

London: November 11th.
"Old Bill" at the Cenotaph.

COPYRIGHT PHOTO
PUBLISHED BY

SAMUELS LTD.
STRAND
LONDON, W.C.2.

The Grave of the Unknown Warrior was unveiled on 11 November 1920 in Westminster Abbey. The idea of exhuming the body of an unidentified soldier and bringing him 'home' for burial in the house of kings and poets was the idea of Army Chaplain, Major David Railton MC. He had been serving in France and had been appalled by the loss and suffering caused by the war. Once he came across a grave marked with a wooden cross marked 'An unknown British Soldier, of the Black Watch'. He was moved by the thought that this man, whoever he was, had a family back home who would never know where he was buried. He wrote later how he thought: 'Let this body – this symbol of him – be carried reverently over the sea to his native land.'[5]

The King approved of the idea. Four bodies of unidentified men were exhumed from four different battlefields at Ypres, Arras, the Somme and the Aisne, where units of the Royal Naval division, as well as the Army and Royal Air Force, had died. These were placed in coffins and at midnight on 7 November Brigadier General Louis Wyatt, General Officer Commanding British Forces in France and Flanders, entered the tent and, blindfolded, chose one of the four. This was then placed in a special coffin, made from two-inch-thick oak from a tree that had grown in Hampton Court Palace Garden, and brought back to Britain with full military honours.

On 11 November 1920, the coffin was placed on a gun carriage drawn by six black horses of the Royal Horse Artillery and began its journey through the streets lined with crowds. As it arrived in Whitehall, King George V unveiled the Cenotaph and placed a wreath of red roses

Far left: George V laying a wreath at the unveiling of the Cenotaph, 11 November 1920.

Left: George V laying a wreath of roses and bay on the coffin of the Unknown Warrior in Whitehall.

Left: The coffin of the Unknown Warrior at Westminster Abbey, 11 November 1920.

Above: The Grave in the Abbey today.

Opposite: Remembrance Day Service at the Cenotaph in Whitehall, 1929.

Above: Laurence Binyon, English poet, dramatist and scholar, best known for his poem 'For the Fallen'.

Right: A Scouts group at the Cenotaph in Whitehall, Remembrance Day 1941.

and bay on the coffin. The carriage then progressed to Westminster Abbey with escorting pall bearers from the highest offices in the Army, Navy and Royal Air Force, including Field Marshal Earl Haig. It entered Westminster Abbey through the north door and the coffin was laid to rest in soil from France. It is estimated that in the week after the internment more than 1.25 million people filed past the tomb to pay their respects. The Grave of the Unknown Warrior had become a grave for every family without one in a war cemetery.

Following the decision to adopt the poppy as a symbol in September 1921, Earl Haig announced that he wished 11 November 1921 to be known as Remembrance Day. His wish was granted, and the formal Act of Remembrance was developed into the basic framework we know today.

The Service of Remembrance has two simple components at its heart. First, four lines of a poem, 'For the Fallen', written in 1914 by Laurence Binyon, an English poet, dramatist and art scholar, known within the Legion as the Exhortation, are read out:

They shall grow not old, as we that are left grow old;
Age shall not weary them, nor the years condemn.
At the going down of the sun and in the morning
We will remember them.

The second is the Two Minute Silence, which was suggested by Sir Percy Fitzpatrick, a South African author and politician, in honour of the dead. He proposed the idea to the King who immediately ordered that it should be held at 11am on 11 November 1919. As Big Ben struck 11 all activity in the capital stopped, as it did in towns and cities all over Britain. The next day *The Manchester Guardian* described the scene:

The main streets were filled with people as eleven o'clock drew near. Many had come especially to be present on a unique occasion. It was remarkable with what quickness all noise was hushed when the dull explosion of the first maroon was heard. Horses were pulled up, tramcars stopped still where they stood, carts and motor-cars and pedestrians were as if suddenly fixed to the ground.

Today at the Cenotaph, as Big Ben strikes 11, the Two Minute Silence commences. The end is marked by a bugler sounding Last Post. This service is repeated all over the country, and further afield, in churches and at war memorials. There are variations on the other aspects of the service that top and tail the occasion, but the Exhortation and the Two Minute Silence are always there.

The National Service of Remembrance at the Cenotaph has evolved over the years. The Bishop of London leads the prayers and then wreaths of poppies are laid at the foot of the Cenotaph, starting with Her

Majesty The Queen, now represented by Prince Charles, and then other members of the Royal Family, politicians and guests from other nations, and heads of the different branches of the Armed Forces. Once the Royals depart it falls to the Legion to organise the stirring and emotional march past of 10,000 UK and Commonwealth veterans of all ages. They take a royal salute out of the public eye on Horse Guards Parade at the end of the march. It is a solemn, respectful and perfectly choreographed ceremony that is watched by millions at home and abroad. But who organises it? The Queen's Privy Council asks the monarch every year if it can organise a Service of Remembrance. Once permission is granted it is organised by the Ministry of Defence, the Foreign, Commonwealth & Development Office and the Department for Digital, Culture, Media & Sport. This august group has the responsibility for the ceremony and the wreath-laying. As the royal party and distinguished guests depart it becomes a Legion event.

When the ceremony was first organised in the early 1920s it was still in development. In 1927 the Legion was put in charge of getting ex-Servicemen to Whitehall and that year there were ten times as many men at the Cenotaph as there had been in previous years. Today the capacity for the march past is 10,000 but the Legion receives requests from all manner of bodies asking for permission to join the ceremony and even now there are many more people hopeful of being part of the event than the Legion, and London, can cope with.

Any ex-Serviceman or woman who is scheduled to attend the National Service of Remembrance can hail a participating Poppy Cab at one of the agreed points at stations around the capital and find him or herself transported there and back for free. The cost of this service is supported by the Legion, which gives the Taxi

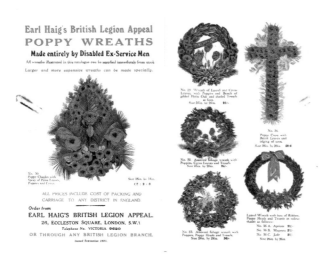

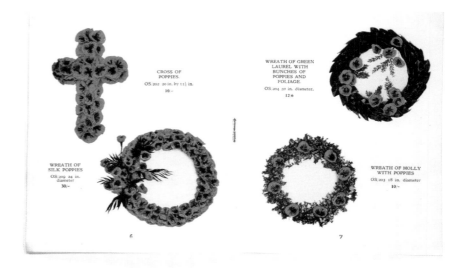

Opposite: Her Majesty The Queen, laying her wreath at the Cenotaph, 1954.

Above: This pamphlet, dating from 1931, advertises poppy wreaths for sale with designs to suit every purse.

Charity for Military Veterans an annual grant. It is one of the most popular ways of helping veterans to get to and from the Cenotaph, as well as to other Remembrance Services in Normandy, Holland and Belgium. The taxi drivers, some of whom had been through the Legion's Taxi School, see it as a way to pay back part of the debt owed to the veterans old and young.

The Remembrance Day Service, which became Remembrance Sunday after the Second World War, is held in all corners of the world where Commonwealth troops came from. New Zealand and Australia hold Remembrance Day on 25 April, which marks the day on which men from those two countries entered their first battles on Gallipoli. When the Legion published its annual reports after the Poppy Day Appeals in the 1920s, they often included photographs of Remembrance Services where Legion branches were active. In 1923 there were

images from Tanganyika and Durban; a few years later a photograph of a large service in Kingston, Jamaica, was featured as was a picture of Poppy Collectors in Kenya. Those served as a reminder to Legion members in Britain that they had comrades all over the world.

Until 1923 the wreaths laid at the Cenotaph were floral but that year the idea of a poppy wreath, or at least one that was predominantly made of poppies, was introduced and that tradition has stuck. The wreaths were made at the Poppy Factory and over the next few years the designs developed, some of which were very elaborate. Each senior member of the Royal Family has worked with the Poppy Factory to design his or her own personal wreath. Over the years different designs have become fixed to certain organisations or people but the basic wreath is round and made up of poppies with a central circle for a regimental or organisation badge.

THE FESTIVAL OF REMEMBRANCE

Two major changes that entered national consciousness happened in 1927. The first was permission granted to the BBC to broadcast the Service of Remembrance on the radio. The second was the Festival of Remembrance held for the first time that year, on 11 November, at the Royal Albert Hall. The early broadcasts no longer exist but later ones remind the listener of the extraordinary impact of the Two Minute Silence when more than 10,000 people gathered at the Cenotaph fall silent.

The Royal Albert Hall Festival of Remembrance was proposed by the *Daily Express* in 1927. The paper suggested an evening function with a rally of ex-Servicemen to be broadcast on the BBC. The Legion agreed to this and the first event was organised by the newspaper. Prior to that, starting in 1923, on the evening of Remembrance Day, there had been a performance of John Foulds' *A World Requiem* at the Royal Albert Hall, which was by all accounts a sombre occasion. The new format was to be more of a community celebration with popular songs from the war years. The 1927 evening was oversubscribed and those veterans lucky enough to get tickets thronged together in excitement and clouds of cigarette smoke. A journalist from the *Daily Express* wrote of the festival: 'Words cannot describe – they can only suggest – the scene in the Albert Hall on Armistice night. There has never been anything like it in the history of reunion.

Below, left: The Festival of Remembrance at the Royal Albert Hall, 1936. The backdrop is Tezze British Cemetery in Italy.

Above: Promotion for John Foulds' *A World Requiem*, first performed at the Royal Albert Hall in 1923.

Right: Covers from the Festival of Remembrance at the Royal Albert Hall: (right) 1927; (far right, top to bottom) 1928, 1936 and 1963.

Ten thousand Englishmen, bound by the mightiest memories of our time, met together to sing to the world the songs they sang from hell.'[6]

The Royal Albert Hall was decked with flags hung from the roof, some of them shredded in battle. Over the Royal Box was draped the Union Jack that had flown over the Menin Gate in Ypres during the four years of the war.

Thirteen years fell from us. We ceased to see the Albert Hall and the thousands of faces white in the arc lights; we looked into an abyss of memories where the long columns passed and repassed over the dusty roads of France, where the grotesque, unthinkable things of war happened day and night – the brief joys, the sharp sorrows of those days, the insane injustices of Fate, and above it all, the memory of the men we knew so well, men better than we were, nobler, finer, more worthy of life, who slipped into the silence of death.[7]

When their Patron, the Prince of Wales, entered the hall in civilian dress and a row of medals on his chest, the men, wearing their Flanders Field poppies, stood up and greeted him with cheers and sang 'For he's a jolly good fellow'. The band of the Grenadier Guards struck up the chords of wartime songs which the crowd belted out until they were almost hoarse. When the Prince could reply, he told his audience, 'We must think and speak of peace.'

At the end of the evening the entire audience, led by the Prince, marched to the Cenotaph carrying torches, and were joined by other ex-Servicemen who had been in Hyde Park to hear the ceremony broadcast. Members of the public fell in with the crowd and the evening ended with the torch bearers making a ring around the Cenotaph. It had been a great success but the officers of the Legion had worried about the Prince's safety as crowds of well-wishers pressed towards him along the route.

WE ARE THE LEGION

The following year the Legion's General Secretary, Colonel Heath, took responsibility for the evening and there was no repeat of the march. The festival had been so popular that it immediately became part of Remembrancetide. It is wholly the responsibility of the Legion and over time has developed and innovated to reflect its current thinking. In 1953 the festival was televised for the first time and, although few households had television sets, the broadcast became an annual tradition. The festival has been themed to mark anniversaries: 1928, 1968, 2018 and, from the Second World War, D-Day '25, '50, '75. In 2014 a solemn service commemorated the outbreak of the First World War; in 2018 the magnificent festival that marked the end of that war won the Live Event category at the British Academy of Film and Television Arts (BAFTA) Awards in May 2019. That autumn, when Sheku Kanneh-Mason played 'Hallelujah', the television audience was estimated to be 7.5 million with countless others joining on digital platforms around the world.

In 1928, for the tenth anniversary of the end of the First World War, the Royal Albert Hall was decorated with an aisle of sandbags that led across the length of the oval arena to a dugout behind which stretched a huge Union Jack that went from floor to ceiling. A great hush came over the audience when Royal Red Cross Sisters passed in 'stately file' along the sandbagged road dividing the arena. The inclusion of representatives of the women's Forces and other organisations has been a theme ever since.

In November 1971 the Legion marked its 50th anniversary and celebrated its new status as the Royal British Legion. There was an innovation in the form of an introductory programme of music by the Legion's Military Band with a muster of Legion standards alongside those of the Armed Forces.

A highpoint of the annual Festival of Remembrance is the arrival of Her Majesty The Queen and the entire retinue of senior members of the Royal Family, which is announced by the Royal Fanfare. The festival is the only feature of British life that regularly brings the senior Royal Family together. The Queen first attended the Festival of Remembrance as Princess Elizabeth in 1945 and has missed only two services since then.

Over the decades the Legion has produced ever more ambitious and stunning sets, but the evening follows the same format. There is music from one of the household bands, readings, musical performances by stars from the world of entertainment, parades and drills by serving men and women, and of course the presence of veterans. Then the moving scene of 500 men and women from the Armed Forces and some civilian services coming down the steps into the great oval to stand for the Act of Remembrance. As Last Post is sounded and the Two Minute Silence has the audience in its thrall, a million crepe poppies fall silently from the ceiling onto the audience below, resting indiscriminately on caps, heads, shoulders. The idea for the Poppy Drop is almost as old as the Festival of Remembrance itself and was introduced in 1929 when the Exhortation, the four lines of Binyon's 'For the Fallen', were used for the first time.

THE FIELD OF REMEMBRANCE

The tenth anniversary of the end of the First World War gave birth to another tradition around 11 November. Major George Howson proposed a Field of Remembrance on the lawn outside St Margaret's Church, Westminster, close to the Abbey and the final resting place of the Unknown Warrior. Howson

and his wife took a group of disabled men from the Poppy Factory to Westminster. There they stood with collecting tins and encouraged members of the public to buy a poppy from the men and plant it around an original wooden battlefield cross that had been replaced in France by an Imperial War Graves Commission headstone. People passing by were intrigued and stopped to ask questions of the men with the poppies. It quickly caught on and the first Field of Remembrance was a sea of red poppies waving in the breeze. Three years later one of the men at the factory designed a little wooden stake with a poppy at its centre. Those were sold to people who wished to dedicate personal messages by writing on the crosses before they were planted. It was so popular that the lawns had to be divided up into plots for the Army, Navy and Royal Air Force.

For the families of those whose men died and were buried abroad there was still a desire to do something more personal than buying a poppy and standing in silence at the local war memorial on 11 November. The Legion listened to its members and once the designs of wreaths had been settled it began to advertise a service for bereaved families. They could choose a wreath to suit their financial situation and these would be made for them in the Poppy Factory in Richmond and shipped out to Ypres. There, members of the Legion in Belgium and France would take them to cemeteries or memorials and, following a short Act of Remembrance at which any message from the family is read out, lay them on behalf of the families. The wreaths could have a message attached and thus a more intimate memorial to a fallen son or father or brother could be made. This practice is continued by Legion members overseas to this day.

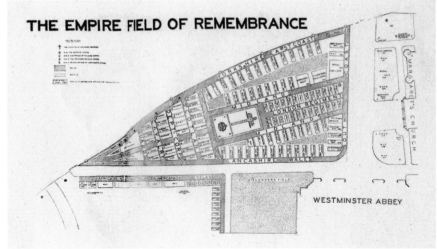

THE EMPIRE FIELD OF REMEMBRANCE

WESTMINSTER ABBEY

Opposite: The Field of
Remembrance outside
Westminster Abbey,
1930, and the layout of
the field as shown in the
*Journal, c.*1930.

Right: A First World War
veteran plants a poppy in
the Field of Remembrance,
*c.*1930.

REMEMBRANCE

Opposite: Poppy stakes in
the Field of Remembrance.

Above, left to right: The
Field of Remembrance has
evolved over the years, but
the message remains the
same: Honour the Fallen.

Remembrance is not only about 11 November. Over the years there have been Acts of Remembrance and pilgrimages all over the world, many organised by the Legion. The largest ever was the Great Pilgrimage to France and Belgium in August 1928. At the invitation of the French, the National Executive Committee began to consider how a major event might be organised. The Great Pilgrimage was planned to take place on the tenth anniversary of the so-called '100 days' that marked the battles which led to the end of the First World War. Earl Haig was behind the idea of this huge undertaking and wished that the climax of the visit, the ceremony at the Menin Gate Memorial, should take place on 8 August, the date of the first of those defining battles. Sadly, Haig's death in January 1928 robbed the pilgrims of the honour of marching through the Menin Gate and past their President and wartime leader.

Haig had made it clear that he wanted to keep the costs of the pilgrimage within the means of the working man or war widow, so he asked those tasked with the organisation to get as much help in kind as possible from the French and Belgians. In the end the cost per head was £4 6s (£250). Train companies in Britain, France and Belgium offered discounted fares and the accommodation on the continent was provided by the hosts in a variety of hotels and private houses. The French were astonished and impressed that there was equality between the ranks, and families were delighted to meet what they described as the real working man. It did lead to the odd anomalous situation when, for example, 75-year-old General Sir Ian Hamilton, Scottish President of the Legion, found himself quartered in Arras in a room with a small bed for both him and

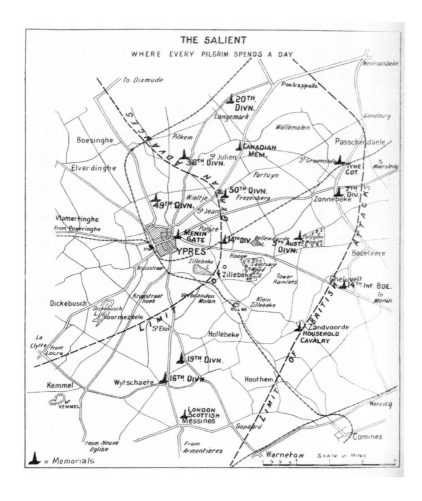

The Salient map. "THE SALIENT — WHERE EVERY PILGRIM SPENDS A DAY"

Lieutenant General Sir Edward Bethune, who was 73. Hamilton, who had a delicious sense of humour, said on a radio interview after the trip: 'I never expected a soft time, but community sleeping was more than I had bargained for.' A second bed was procured for the two generals.

The Great Pilgrimage was planned to the last detail by Major James Harter. Month after month instructions were published in the *Journal* informing would-be pilgrims of setting-off points, train timetables, accommodation, cemetery visits and battlefield tours as well as advising on suitable footwear. Colonel Crosfield, the Legion's Chairman at the time, wrote in the January 1928 *Journal* of how the pilgrimage should not be regarded 'merely as a visit to the War Graves Cemeteries; it is a collective fulfilment of part of that solemn pledge, not of words but of actual faith, between comrades, that those who might survive the

Opposite: 11,000 veterans, widows and orphans attended the ceremony at the Menin Gate Memorial at Ypres on the Great Pilgrimage of 1928.

Above and right: The Great Pilgrimage was organised with military precision. Participants had maps, tickets and a detailed itinerary.

great ordeal would see that the dead were cared for, and the interest of the widows and children secured'.

In all, 11,000 veterans and widows, including 2,000 Standard Bearers, crossed the Channel on 5 August and made their way by train and coach to the battlefields of the Somme. Many veterans recognised features in the landscape as they moved through the countryside. For some it was overwhelming: 'When the British Cemeteries came into sight, and were saluted as we passed, men stared hard and gulped, and furtively wiped away tears which could not be checked.' Others brought the familiar black humour of the British soldier to the fore. 'A stalwart on crutches gazed thoughtfully towards Beaumont Hamel and said: "I wonder if my blinkin' leg is still up there?"'[8] The trench system was still clear to see and men stopped and reminisced about those who had not come home and whose final resting places they could now visit in peace.

From there they moved to Vimy Ridge, which the Canadians had captured from the Germans in April 1917. There too the trench systems were visible and the pilgrims were able to get a view of the landscape around Thélus and imagine for themselves the chaos of the battlefields of almost a dozen years earlier. And then to Ypres for the magnificent ceremony at the Menin Gate Memorial.

The Menin Gate is the Commonwealth War Graves Commission's largest war memorial in Belgium and bears the names of 54,000 soldiers of the former British Empire who died on battlefields of the Ypres Salient and whose bodies were unidentified. The number was so great that the remaining 11,000 had to be inscribed on the walls at the vast cemetery at Tyne Cot. The Menin Gate Memorial was designed by Sir Reginald Blomfield, one of the three architects who worked in France and

Belgium after the war. It was unveiled in July 1927,
a year before the Great Pilgrimage, having taken four
years to build.

From 1928 members of the Last Post Association in
Ypres have sounded Last Post daily at 8pm. Today the
ceremony is attended by hundreds, often thousands,
of people who visit the cemeteries and memorials in the
area. Parties of schoolchildren can be seen standing next
to veterans and groups of tourists who happen to be in
the square when the crowds start to gather. In the past
the ceremony was not as popular and occasionally there
would be one or two locals in addition to the members
of the Association. The only time the ceremony has been
missed until now was over the four years of the German
occupation of Belgium from 1940 to 1944.

The Ypres Salient is the resting place of some
250,000 British and Commonwealth Servicemen.

It is estimated that one in four of those who fell in the
war is buried or commemorated in or around Ypres.
Naturally, the town and its great memorial became the
heart of battlefield pilgrimages and commemorations.
On that fine, sunny day in August 1928, those who
were there were only too aware of the sacrifice those
men had made. E F Pinnington wrote in the *Journal*
about the parade and ceremony at Ypres:

For here indeed the bitter cup of Remembrance was
soon to overflow. Here, indeed, Grief was to take
up the harp and smite on every chord. At Cambrai,
at Beaumont-Hamel, at Vimy, at all the other places
visited, there was always something to assuage the
poignancy of sorrow stirred by those memorials and
those resting places of our dead. But here at Ypres
there was nothing, nothing at all. 'Tis true, the city

is no longer the battered Wipers of our Service days, but a modern, up-to-date town, snug and flourishing. But to the heart of the pilgrim, attuned to sadness, the Cloth Hall itself seemed to be the embodiment of the Ypres as it was in the days of Hell Fire Corner and the shambles of the Menin Road.

It was a solemn but beautiful, colourful occasion held under a clear sky and watched by thousands of French and Belgian well-wishers who had been following the pilgrims' progress around the battlefields. There were hymns, prayers and an address by the Archbishop of York who spoke of memories revived, sometimes painfully, having been locked away for a decade. His thoughts on these memories are captured in the September 1928 *Journal*: 'Yet, surely, something of their bitterness is taken from them when you behold the skies you once saw ablaze with the fires and shaken by the thunder of war looking down on peaceful homes and fields once scarred and blasted and dark with the shadow of death now glowing with the gold of harvest.'

As the bugler sounded Last Post, 2,000 standards dipped for the Two Minute Silence and as Reveille sent out its challenging call of optimism, the standards raised again. Everyone cradled his or her own private thoughts and memories of the long years of war and the loss of family, friends and comrades. In the commemorative book written that autumn the description of the service conveys a little of the raw emotion that was felt by all those present: 'For the moment we leave 11,000 bowed and sobbing pilgrims to commune with their loved ones; we stand bare-headed while the "Last Post" is sounded, and, after a short pause, proudly raise our heads at the "Reveille". Surely, the Archbishop of

York was right when he said, "Lest we forget". Those of us who attended the service will never forget.'

For the 1,600 widows, mothers, daughters and sisters who had joined the pilgrimage it was especially poignant to see the battlefields where their men had died and to visit the exquisitely tended cemeteries where they lay. One widow wore the ribbons of two Victoria Crosses that had been awarded to her husband and her son. Both had died. Another woman, described as a proud but sad mother, wore 12 medals. She had lost three sons in the war: two on the Ypres Salient and one on the Aisne.

The Great Pilgrimage exceeded all expectations and everyone who wrote of it, including the Prince of Wales, spoke of the exceptional comradeship and cooperation that had been evident from the minute the pilgrims set off from home. Colonel Crosfield wrote in the *Journal* with satisfaction: 'The Pilgrimage has brought consolation to the bereaved, has renewed good fellowship between ourselves and our Allies, and has reminded the world of the immense sacrifices of the British Empire in the War.'

Crosfield had been to Paris to light the flame of Remembrance on the Tomb of the Unknown Soldier at the Arc de Triomphe before joining the pilgrimage. Major Brunel Cohen had been invited to Brussels to lay a wreath at the Tomb of the Unknown Soldier there. That evening he gave an address on Belgian radio in which he thanked the Belgians for keeping up the tradition of sounding Last Post at the Menin Gate Memorial every evening at sundown. That had struck a chord with the Belgian people and the next day he was cheered as he drove his electric wheelchair at the head of the march past in Ypres. All along the line the crowd shouted out 'Vive le Commandant Cohen!' as he went by.

REMEMBRANCE AFTER 1945

After the Second World War, when a further 600,000 soldiers, sailors and airmen were added to the ranks of those lost in war and 67,200 British civilians had died, the Legion had to ask itself how to reflect the new situation. It was decided that Remembrance Day should be renamed Remembrance Sunday to honour the dead of both world wars and should be observed on the Sunday closest to 11 November, or on 11 November itself if it fell on a Sunday. At the same time the Poppy Day Appeal was renamed the Poppy Appeal. Then came the further wars of the 20th and early 21st centuries, including Korea, the Suez Crisis, the Troubles in Northern Ireland (which lasted for 30 years), the Falklands War, Bosnia, Kosovo, the two Gulf Wars, and the war in Afghanistan. All these conflicts and many others less familiar had deaths, casualties and bereaved families. They too needed the support of the Legion and they also needed to be included in the Festival and Act of Remembrance. In 2000 it was decided that their names should be commemorated on a new Armed Forces Memorial that was to be created at the National Memorial Arboretum in Staffordshire (see Chapter 7).

Each year at Remembrancetide the Legion runs a campaign to raise awareness of its continuing responsibility towards the ex-Service community and their families. It would be all too easy for the message to become repetitive, but the Legion is a master at judging the times, as we saw from the Poppy Popsies of the 1970s. Since the 1990s it has been determined to focus on the men and women who have been involved in conflict and war in more recent years and to bring them into the Remembrance story. Sometimes the

After a week of heavy thunderstorms and torrential rain across the country, Saturday 15 August 2020 dawned bright in Staffordshire with light-grey clouds scudding briskly overhead. Guests, looking self-conscious in face masks, began arriving early in the morning, including veterans from the 14th Army, the Chindits, prisoners of war of the Japanese and civilian internees, as well as family members and representatives from all branches of today's Armed Forces. The atmosphere was a mixture of joyful celebration, quiet reflection and not a little nervousness. This small, socially distanced gathering reflected the great communities across the world who could not be present. As the military band struck up 'We'll Meet Again' there was an audible intake of breath followed by a sense that this was familiar, despite the strangeness of life under the coronavirus pandemic.

Just after 10.40am the Royal Party arrived. Prince Charles and the Duchess of Cornwall took their seats on a bench beside a section of the Thailand–Burma Railway and the service began, introduced by the actor Art Malik, whose father had fought with the 14th Army. Representatives of all parts of the Commonwealth contributed to the event, which culminated in the Two Minute Silence. The live broadcast included the laying of wreaths at cemeteries and memorials, many of them Commonwealth War Graves Commission sites, across the world. The reach of the war could not have been more movingly portrayed than in this way. Darbara Singh Bhullar, pictured here next to a section of the Thailand–Burma Railway at the National Memorial Arboretum, was in the Communications Signal Corps in the British Indian Army, fighting against the Japanese in the jungles of Burma between 1944 and 1945.

campaign will focus on a single hero or heroine, such as Flight Lieutenant John Nichol, who was shot down and captured in the Gulf War. He was tortured in prison and before being released he was paraded on Iraqi television causing worldwide condemnation. Similarly, Simon Weston, the soldier burned in the Falklands War, whose bravery in showing his injured face to the world is extraordinary, has been a poster boy for the Legion. As has Colonel Sir Tom Moore who raised over £38 million for the NHS during the coronavirus pandemic in 2020. However, Remembrance is not just about well-known heroes. It also focuses on the less heroic aspect of war. A series of posters in the 1990s showed veterans sleeping on the streets or trapped at home, the war they had fought in playing over and over in their minds. One stark image shows an elderly man in a wheelchair with his back to the camera. The caption reads: '50 years on there are still prisoners of war'.

After the terrorist attacks in London on 7 July 2005 the shape of Remembrance began to change again. This time the first responders were on the scene dealing with the horrific sights and human tragedies that those four bombs had produced. London was under attack for the first time since the Troubles, the assailants this time being Islamist terrorists.

The Legion remains the national champion of Remembrance and is committed to ensuring that it is understood and available to every child and community in the UK. Why does this matter and what is of relevance to the children of the 21st century? Because if we are to forget those who laid down their lives for us, whether in the most recent fights against terrorism or in the distant battles on the Somme, in far-off Burma or on the Falkland Islands, we risk ignoring those who are fighting for our way of life. The Legion believes that understanding our shared heritage of Remembrance helps to bring communities together and ensures that we recognise the service and sacrifice of past and present generations.

Right: Army cadets in Southend in July 2013.

Top, left to right: Colour Sergeant Johnson Beharry VC COG with Chelsea Pensioners at the National Service of Remembrance, Sunday 12 November 2017.

Above, left: 'Eyes Right!' Scottish veterans take Royal Review after the Cenotaph parade.

Above, right: A D-Day veteran enjoying a joke with Flight Lieutenant Mandeep Kaur, the first Sikh padre in the Royal Air Force, 2017.

Dilys Hooper is a passionate member of the Legion who has been involved in one way or another since she was 20 when she volunteered as a collector in the week leading up to Remembrance Sunday. Her father had served in the Royal Navy in the Second World War and impressed on her the importance of honouring 'ordinary people with ordinary lives' who did something brave on behalf of other people and sometimes paid the ultimate price. 'We have to ensure we respect what men and women did for their country and we have to ensure the ex-Service community gets the best it can out of life.' Today she is on the Membership Council with a special remit to represent Youth, and is a powerhouse of ideas for commemoration around Remembrancetide.

Over the past few years she has been involved in an initiative with members of the Women's Institute who knit poppies for schoolchildren in Reception classes. A poppy is given to each child to wear on their school uniform and then to give to their parents as a memento of their first Remembrance Day. It is a simple idea but it taps into a deep sense of commitment from the older generation and a sense of wonder and excitement from the five-year-olds. Dilys said: 'The youth are our future and our custodians of Remembrance. If we don't nurture them now, Remembrance will not follow through.' The children below are from Barnton Community Nursery and Primary School near Northwich in Cheshire.

LEST WE FORGET

Five million men and women from five regions of the Indian subcontinent (Bangladesh, India, Nepal, Pakistan and Sri Lanka), Africa and the Caribbean volunteered to serve with the British Armed Forces during the First and Second World Wars. They fought in almost every theatre of war, seeing action on the Western Front in France and Belgium from 1914, as well as in the Middle East where they fought with distinction against the Turks in the Mesopotamian campaign. Indians served on the Gallipoli peninsula, and others went to East and West Africa, and even to China; 100,000 Gurkhas from Nepal helped to defeat the Germans on the Western Front. Men from many African countries served with the Allied Forces during the First World War, as front-line troops and in auxiliary roles. Participants came from Nigeria, the Gambia, Rhodesia (now Zimbabwe), South Africa, Sierra Leone, Uganda, Nyasaland (now Malawi), Kenya and the Gold Coast (now Ghana). About 55,000 men served as combatant soldiers, and many hundreds of thousands more as carriers or auxiliary troops. An estimated 10,000 were killed or died while serving.

At the outbreak of the Second World War men and women from all over the Indian subcontinent, Africa and the Caribbean again volunteered to serve alongside the British, whether in the Army, the Royal Air Force or the Merchant Navy. Around 6,000 West Indians served in the Royal Air Force and 15,000 in the Merchant Navy, while African countries sent 372,000 men and women to serve with the Allied Forces.

The largest number of volunteers came from the five regions of the Indian subcontinent and comprised the largest volunteer army in history. More than 2.5 million

Above, left: Noor Inayat Khan was a Special Operations Executive (SOE) agent and the first female radio operator to be sent into occupied France. She was captured and executed by the Nazis in 1944.

Above, right: Khudadad Khan VC was the first soldier of the British Indian Army to be awarded the Victoria Cross, on 31 October 1914, for conspicuous bravery.

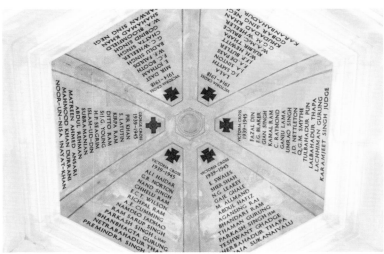

men and women gave their services. Of these, 700,000 served in the 14th Army in Burma, representing nearly three-quarters of its strength, and helped to defeat the Imperial Japanese Army in some of the worst fighting conditions of the war. Indians served in the North African campaign against the Germans; in Eritrea and Abyssinia against the Italians; in Iran and Iraq; and in Italy, where they took part in some of the bloodiest fighting at the Battle of Monte Cassino. Indian, African and Caribbean women took part in their hundreds of thousands, either in the women's services or as nurses or munitions workers, and even a handful were involved in the secret services. Field Marshal Sir Claude Auchinleck, who commanded the Indian Forces in the Middle East, said later that the British 'couldn't have come through both wars if they hadn't had the Indian Army.'

The Memorial Gates are a war memorial in the heart of London commemorating the men and women from the Indian subcontinent, Africa and the Caribbean who gave their lives in the two world wars. The price they paid was enormous: 1.7 million were killed, missing or disabled. Located at the Hyde Park Corner end of Constitution Hill, the Memorial Gates were designed by Liam O'Connor Architects. Four individual Portland stone piers are inscribed with the names of the Commonwealth countries and topped with bronze urns in which flames are lit on special occasions such as Remembrance Sunday, Armistice Day and Commonwealth Day.

Next to the Memorial Gates is the memorial pavilion whose ceiling commemorates those awarded the highest honours in the two world wars. There are the names of 23 Victoria Cross holders from the First World War and 39 from the Second World War along with 12 George Cross holders.

The driving force behind the creation of the Memorial Gates was Baroness Flather, the first Asian woman appointed to the House of Lords, whose father volunteered as a stretcher bearer in Mesopotamia in the First World War. She said in an interview that it was her proudest achievement. The chairman of the Memorial Gates Council, The Lord Bilimoria CBE DL, is clear that this part of British history should be understood and celebrated. He is keen that the younger generations, whose forebears stood and fought for Britain, should be proud of that contribution. He said: 'The memorial has at its heart not only Remembrance of the past but a stake in the future. Young people are a key part of the thinking behind the memorial. Only through their understanding of the proud traditions of duty and sacrifice embodied by all those who volunteered to stand by Britain in the two world wars will those sacred memories have relevance for the future.' Poet Ben Okri's words, inscribed on the memorial, echo this: 'Our future is greater than our past'.

In 2021, marking 100 years of Remembrance, the Legion entered into a formal partnership with the Memorial Gates Trust to enhance its profile, and that of the Commonwealth Day services, and its community outreach and educational materials for young people.

G R
MINISTRY of LABOUR

DISCHARGED
SAILORS & SOLDIERS

Chapter 4

THE LEGION
AT WORK

THE LEGION AT WORK

'Don't Pity a Disabled Man – Find him a Job'. This was one of many slogans on posters produced by the Legion in the 1920s. Thousands of men had returned from the battlefields of France, Belgium and further afield with life-changing disabilities. Many struggled to find employment. There was prejudice against hiring a disabled man over a healthy one, especially when the Great Depression and the economic downturn began to bite, and this was to become a major source of anxiety for men and their families.

Nationally the Legion was determined to do everything it could to help men disabled by the war to get back on their feet. It lobbied for pensions and benefits and tried to encourage self-help where possible but there was no doubt in anyone's minds that nothing was more depressing for a man who had fought for his King and country than not to be able to find work. It was a matter of self-worth and the lack of employment opportunities weighed heavily on those trying to help men to find jobs.

It is hard to imagine from today's perspective how completely abandoned the unemployed were in the 1920s. There were reports in the Legion's *Journal* of men with wives and any number of children living in single rooms in tenement blocks in squalor and with almost no furniture. In the countryside there were

Above: Ex-civil servants protest near the Cenotaph in Whitehall, 1921.

Opposite: Posters were used to highlight the plight of men disabled by war and unable to find work.

families living in sheds and farm buildings, and one family with eight children was housed in a pigsty. Such was the poverty among those who fell on hard times that for some the only option was the workhouse, an institution used during the Victorian era for housing men or women who were unable to support themselves.

By the end of the 19th century, workhouses had become refuges for the older poor who were often sick or infirm. Now there was a new influx into these institutions and the Legion was horrified. There was anger, too, among the returning men who had been promised a 'land fit for heroes' with housing and jobs. The reality was so different. The *Journal* published letter after letter from disillusioned, angry men who felt the government had let them down. The greatest part of their ire was directed at the despised conscientious objectors who, many believed, were sitting in comfortable jobs in the civil service. A man who signed himself 'Disgusted', wrote using italics for emphasis: '*it is an outrageous insult to Britain's heroes* (who fail to discover Lloyd George's promised homes the while). Recently 500 ex-Service men were refused admission to the Wandsworth workhouse, *because of the many hundreds of such men and their families already there!* And in face of that the abominable "Conchie" readily finds employment. *Something is radically wrong.*' This makes uncomfortable reading today, as does the Legion's commitment to getting women to give up their jobs in favour of the returning ex-Servicemen, but it was part and parcel of the world of the 1920s.

Above: Major David Railton MC, c.1917.

Right: Sir Frederick Maurice opening the Limbless and Disabled Ex-Servicemen's Factory at Acton, London, 1933.

Opposite: The Battersea Branch of the Legion established a soup kitchen in 1933 at the request of the Prince of Wales. The Metropolitan Area Chairman, Admiral Sir Henry Bruce (left), and the Mayor pour soup.

Major David Railton MC, the former Army Chaplain who had been inspired to suggest the Grave of the Unknown Warrior in Westminster Abbey, decided to see for himself if the situation for men looking for work was as bad as had been reported to him. He had been born into a prominent Salvation Army family and had always had concern for the poor and homeless. With a shilling in his pocket and a letter offering him a job in a town many miles away from his home in York, he set off on foot in the autumn of 1921 to try to work his way to the town. It was a depressing experience. At every town and village, at workshops, factory doors and on farms, he heard the same message: 'Nothin' doin', lad.' Some men were angry with him for trying to find work on their patch; most were sympathetic; and those looking for work, like he was, were down and out, desperate. He spent a night in a dosshouse in the company of unemployed men and wrote of the experience in the 1922 *Journal*: 'No one who has ever seen it will forget the silent despair in the room where the men wait before the whistle goes for bed.' He spent a week on the road, never reaching the town where he had been promised work. For him it was only an experiment but for everyone else he met it was the reality. 'I can still see, when I am sometimes alone, the tragedies of this little adventure. I intend to help the British Legion in removing them. If the British Legion doesn't do it, nobody else will.'

At branch level the welfare teams saw this playing out for real, day in, day out. They did what they could to support families of disabled and unemployed men in their area. There was help from the government in the form of National Insurance but the allowance was only about one-third of an average wage and was not available to agricultural workers or the self-employed, who relied on the Poor Law that was administered at a local level. The Legion estimated there were some 35,000 ex-Service family members in Poor Law institutions in 1924.[9] In a further twist, there was no relief at all for officers, who were presumed to be able to support themselves through independent means. However, battlefield promotions meant this was not always the case and it was something that had deeply concerned Earl Haig. He had been the driving force behind the Officers' Association, which was set up in 1920 to help officers who found themselves in straitened circumstances after the war.

Branches of the Women's Section set up soup kitchens in the East End of London and other deprived areas to help feed the unemployed and their dependants. Local relief committees could help hardship cases with vouchers for necessities such as meat, groceries or coal for heating. In 1923 the Legion's branches recorded nearly 250,000 cases of help from the funds. Earl Haig published a plan for

an annual amount that needed to be raised from the Poppy Day Appeal to support the welfare the Legion was committed to. He wrote in the December 1921 *Journal*: 'Among the 7 million men who fought in the Great War and the wives and children of the 1 million dead or missing, it is estimated that one in every hundred, or 70,000 in all, needs help in some form or another.' He estimated that the average amount required was £25 (£1,200), which would mean that the appeal would need to raise £1.75 million (£90 million). 'Money, and an adequate amount of money, is necessary to tide warriors over their bad times, since all cannot immediately be placed in permanent employment.'

GIVE THE MAN A LOAN

From the earliest days the Legion advertised a fund for loans to be made available for enterprising business start-ups. It was part of the British Legion Unity Relief Fund, which had three objectives: to relieve distress among ex-Servicemen and their dependants; to help men find employment through approved employment schemes; and to provide loans for men who wanted to start or further their own businesses. The fund was kickstarted with a grant of £150,000 (£7.3 million) from the Prince of Wales and a further £30,000 (£1.4 million) from other sources. Applications had to include a proper business plan and were scrutinised by the branches, with help from local businessmen. The loans were capped at £25 and were designed to help men set up small businesses such as window cleaning or boot repairs. A loan of £5 could help a man start a grocery business; £20 could buy a horse and cart. The *Journal* reported on good-news stories, such

Above and opposite, top: A fruit and vegetable stall and boot repair shop established by ex-Servicemen using Legion funds.

Above: This shop was established in 1927 by an ex-Serviceman and his wife with money from the Unity Relief Fund.

as a painting and decorating business set up by one man in London that was so successful in the first six months of its existence it required extra capital in order to expand to meet demand. In Hampshire one branch launched a handyman scheme. The branch supplied the tools, paid for by the fund, and a dozen men were able to make a living doing jobbing work around the town. In January 1922, the editor was delighted to report that 13 disabled men had been employed by a workshop to make toys.

Other men applied for small loans to open shops selling goods, from haberdashery to fruit and vegetables. The loans were interest free but had to be repaid in regular payments. It was a small exercise in terms of the numbers of men needing to find paid employment but for those it helped it was a great boost to their confidence and morale. The editor of the *Journal* published a monthly suggestion on careers for ex-Servicemen. These ranged from poultry-keeping to becoming a travelling salesman. Another suggestion was to buy a lorry and become a delivery driver. The first edition of the *Journal*, published in July 1921, suggested a career in the movies either as a cinema projectionist or in film production. This latter turned out to be wishful thinking, but it shows the energy behind the early contributors to the *Journal*.

After the Second World War the Legion's focus was on getting men into work and ensuring the government stuck to its quota of employing 3 per cent of disabled men into the workforce. The small grants were temporarily replaced with housing loans for people who were badly housed, reflecting one of the great challenges of the post-war world. The small-business scheme was reintroduced in 1985 and loans of up to £2,500 over five years were available. About 150 were

taken up annually and used to start up anything from
a boarding kennel to a gym and, later, a computer-
software installation company. In addition there were
schemes to give men training in a specialist trade. One
beneficiary was the late Sean Connery. In 1946 he
joined the Royal Navy and spent three years training to
be an anti-aircraft crewman. Aged 19, he was medically
discharged on a disability pension of 6s 8d a week
on account of an ulcer. After taking a number of jobs
he joined a Legion scheme to help the young and
disabled. He chose to train as a French polisher and it
was while working in the profession that he got a job
backstage in the theatre. Here he found his true calling
as an actor and a dozen years later he landed the role
of James Bond in *Dr No*.

WELFARE IN THE 21ST CENTURY

Some 60,000 people contact the Legion annually
asking for welfare-related information and support.
About half of the enquiries can be dealt with over
the phone but the other half are passed on to area
teams who carry out an in-depth assessment of
need. The Legion provides specialist services that
can for example help elderly or injured veterans
live independently or provide assistance to people
needing help to manage rent arrears or debts. In
addition, where necessary, caseworkers can award
an individual grant that can alleviate a range of
practical needs. When the coronavirus pandemic
began in early 2020 the Legion, which works closely
with foodbanks nationwide, announced it would
stop sending people to the banks but instead
issue them with food vouchers redeemable at local
supermarkets. This at once freed up foodbanks to
deal with the large increase in numbers of people
using them but it also ensured that ex-Service
personnel in need of help with groceries would
not go hungry.

Antony Baines, Director of Operations at the Legion
since 2012, summed up the Legion's role: 'Once you
have served in the Armed Forces you have the Legion
watching your back for the rest of your life. No matter

when you served, nor whether you were injured in warfare, you get our support.'[10] When a request for help comes to the Legion's welfare teams, the Legion conducts a full assessment to see what the wider needs of that person might be. It conducts a holistic assessment including financial status, housing requirements and connections to family and friends. Such assessments enable important additional information to be revealed. For example, in 2018 a man who initially requested only a new fridge was fully assessed and found to be suffering from a Service-related condition that had had a negative impact on his quality of life. The Legion was able to chase up his appeal and he ended up with a substantial payment that completely changed his life.

The Legion is concerned not only with the financial and housing situation of individuals, but with isolation and loneliness, physical and mental well-being. The Legion has 1,100 welfare staff, including 750 staff in its six Poppy Homes, which cater for elderly ex-Service personnel. They also offer end-of-life care. There is a body of 400 volunteers and the annual budget for welfare is over £100 million.

In addition, there are grants to get men and women back into work or to help them upgrade their skills. Up to £250 can be awarded to a former member of the Armed Forces who needs to apply for a licence to find or continue in work. An example of this might be a Security Industry Authority licence. Up to £1,000 is available to an ex-Serviceman or woman who is seeking work or who is underemployed and needs help to train for a new qualification or travel to attend such training. This grant can also cover childcare and medical expenses.

Left and above: Today Galanos House is one of the Legion's specialist residential homes, which provide both long- and short-term care to members of the Armed Forces community and their dependants.

SIR BENN JACK BRUNEL COHEN KBE

One of the Legion's greatest campaigners was Major Sir Benn Jack Brunel Cohen MP. Born in Liverpool in 1886, Cohen entered the family retail business in 1903. He joined the 1st Volunteer Battalion of the King's Liverpool Regiment and was posted to the Western Front in early 1917; on 31 July, during the Third Battle of Ypres, he sustained severe wounds from machine gun fire and had to have both his legs amputated above the knee. Fitted with prosthetic limbs, he was able to walk short distances on his sticks but was usually seen in his electric wheelchair or in his adapted car.

Cohen used his position as the Conservative MP for Liverpool Fairfield to campaign for disabled ex-Servicemen and all people with disabilities. In his maiden speech he urged that men disabled by their war service should be taught a trade and helped to find a job. In July 1919, he raised a parliamentary question asking why wounded ex-Servicemen were to be excluded from the Victory Parade.

Cohen attended the Unity Conference in 1920 as a representative of the Officers' Association. When the Legion came into being, he became the first Honorary Treasurer, a post he held until 1946 with one break in 1930–2 when he was appointed Vice Chairman.

Cohen was an active member of many of the Legion's delegations in search of peace in the 1930s and was involved in the Poppy Factory, the Legion's Taxi School and with the Women's Section. He was also a keen water-skier and had a special board designed so that he could sit on it behind a motorboat and enjoy the same thrill as his friends. Cohen was knighted in 1943 and was appointed as KBE in 1948. He died in 1965.

The emigration scheme of the British Empire Services League (BESL) was a flagship project in the late 1920s. Ex-Servicemen and their families who fancied a major challenge could apply to leave Britain for a new life in Canada. The scheme was devised to encourage 'Empire migration' by ex-Servicemen who would bring skills to develop agriculture. Earl Haig, who was Patron of the BESL, was enthusiastic in his support. In a speech delivered in Manchester in December 1922 he said:

The British Empire Service League has put forward as one of its main objects the question of *'Reciprocity'*, namely that every ex-Service man, whether he be British born, or born in one of the Dominions or Colonies, belongs not to any one of these, but to the British Empire as a whole and that, wherever he moves in this great Empire of ours, he is welcome as a friend and a brother.

There were four government centres in Britain where the men who applied to go to Canada were trained in all aspects of agriculture. This covered stock and crops, upkeep and repair of agricultural equipment, handling and adjusting harnesses for teams of horses and dealing with minor ailments in cattle. Their wives were taught how to milk a cow, make butter and keep poultry. The training started at 6am and ended at dusk, to emulate the conditions they would encounter in their new country. The course organisers at Chiseldon in Wiltshire set up a creche for the younger children so that their mothers could complete the training. It was a requirement of the scheme that only families or husbands and wives were sent out to Canada. The course lasted six months and the Legion paid for the training, board and lodging, and gave each family 7s 6d a week pocket money. Once the course was over the Legion covered the costs of emigration and settlement in Canada. An assessment of the clothing requirements for the families shocked the welfare officers. Some families had so little that the Women's Section had to supply them with the absolute basics including underwear, boots and warm blankets as well as cold-weather clothing for the bitter Canadian winters. Twenty-one families completed the first round of training.

The pilot scheme saw the families sail from Southampton for a new life in Canada in 1926. They were seen off by the Vice Chairman Colonel Crosfield, Major Cohen, the Mayor of Southampton and the Lord Lieutenant of Hampshire. Standard Bearers from local branches lined the gangway and, according to the *Journal*, 'the band played lively airs'. The photographs of this much-publicised event show the men smiling and cheerful, looking ahead to a bright new future, but some of the wives clutching young children look apprehensive. The *Journal* trumpeted the scheme as one to help families get away from 'poverty, hardship and despair' to a new life of hope and opportunity. On arrival in Canada the families were warmly welcomed by the Canadian Legion and set off to start their new lives.

The reality was much harder for many of them than they had expected. The change from suburban poverty in Britain to working on a smallholding in rural Quebec, Ontario or the Canadian Prairies was tough but they worked at it and in the end 15 of the 21 families succeeded in making a living on their own farms. The next year the scheme took on 50 families and continued to send people to Canada until the unemployment situation there put a stop to emigration in the 1930s. One contented émigré, Charles Littlewood, wrote a

Opposite: British families heading for Canada in 1927 as part of the Legion's Emigration Scheme. The towering figure is National Chairman Fred Lister, part of the official farewell party.

Arthur Beckwith of Crickhowell was a businessman and chairman of the local War Pensions Committee and was untiring in his support of ex-Servicemen. He set up a factory for weaving tweed in Llanwrtyd Wells in 1918 with the idea of giving war-battered men employment in a beautiful area of the country just north of the Brecon Beacons. The mill employed eight disabled ex-Servicemen and three boys who were sons of ex-Servicemen. The wool came from Radnor sheep, a Welsh hill breed with a creamy-white fleece that was soft and ideal for weaving. The dyeing was done on site, as was the spinning, the whole process being conducted under one roof. The Royal Family made a point of supporting the Legion's factory publicly by buying and wearing tartan from the Cambrian Factory as well as making gifts of the woollen products to overseas guests.

In 1927 Beckwith gifted the Cambrian Factory to the Legion, with all the equipment and materials. In 1944 he laid the foundation stone for the extension to the factory, which would provide space to train a further 30 disabled ex-Servicemen.

Llanwrtyd Wells was home not only to the Cambrian Factory but also to a vibrant community and an active branch of the Legion. There was a social club that put on shows and concerts as well as bingo evenings. Although the focus of the factory was on making and selling tweeds, the welfare side was equally important. One manager explained to author Anthony Brown, who was researching a book for the Legion's 50th anniversary, how a disabled mill worker had thanked him for smiling at him on his rounds. 'You don't know what it means to be noticed.'

lengthy letter to Colonel Crosfield in 1927. He described the long hours and the backbreaking nature of farm work but also of his delight in his new world. 'Still, the life is great and the country is greater and the people the greatest people one can wish to meet. First of all let me thank you and the whole of those who have given me and my wife and family this glorious chance.' His wife, who had been a shorthand typist before they left Britain and had never so much as stroked a cow, was now so adept at milking that he was able to go to work for his boss and leave her to manage the homestead during the day. Rees Edwards was equally thrilled with his new life and wrote from Ontario to thank Major Hall, who had taught him agriculture. The September 1927 *Journal* recorded his thanks. 'Believe me, if I'd searched the whole of Canada or the world, for that matter, I'm sure no better located farm could be found. To say that myself and family are happy and quite satisfied with Canada, its people and our own farm in particular, is, to say the least, putting it mild.'

Other families received assistance to go abroad without the need for agricultural training. A sum of £6 (£380) was sufficient to send one man, his wife and nine children to Australia. He was one of 600 men in 1927 alone who emigrated from Britain to Australia, New Zealand, Canada or South Africa. With them went 400 wives and more than 1,000 children. In a separate scheme the Church Army Overseas Settlement Bureau offered the Legion the opportunity to send boys between the ages of 14½ and 17 who had been orphaned by the war to Canada, Australia or New Zealand. There they would be supervised by the Church Army and given employment on farms. This stopped, as did the Canadian agricultural scheme, with the severe economic depression of the early 1930s.

THE LEGION ON THE MOVE

By the late 1920s the motor car became a more familiar sight in Britain. Of the roughly 2 million vehicles on the roads, just under half were privately owned cars, meaning that journeys for pleasure and leisure had become viable. Road deaths were high – some 7,000 in 1934 alone – with pedestrians being half of the victims. Put into context, there were 38.7 million vehicles registered on Britain's roads in 2019 and the road deaths totalled 1,870. In towns and cities, councils had to work out not only how to keep the streets and pavements safe for pedestrians but also what to do about parking cars when people wanted to go shopping or have a night out. In 1927 the Rochdale South Branch of the Legion talked to the town council about the possibility of off-street parking. The council offered the Legion a piece of land free of charge and allowed it to erect a hut and employ two disabled men to act as parking attendants. Thus began a scheme that was to reach throughout England, Wales and Northern Ireland. By 1929 the British Legion Car Park Attendants (Belfast) Ltd had 40 members running car parks throughout the city and in the nearby seaside resorts.

The attendants wore uniforms and took pride in their work. By 1936 Leeds and Harrogate had 58 attendants who were photographed for the *Journal* along with the Mayor and Mayoress of Leeds. This scheme continued successfully in many towns, though not in London, where all car parks were run by the Ministry of Transport. The Car Park Attendants scheme thrived after the Second World War and by the late 1960s was employing over 3,000 men. In 1970 there was an airports division managing the parking facilities at

Above: Printing and binding were just two of the industries at Preston Hall, which later became Royal British Legion Industries (RBLI).

Gatwick and Stansted airports. There was excitement at the time when an experiment was piloted: the Courtesy Car scheme. This was something completely new and the Legion was proud to pioneer it. A bright-green Ford van labelled 'Courtesy Car British Legion Attendants' would buzz around the airport's car parks collecting individuals from their cars and dropping them at the terminals. The cars would then be taken to a secure compound within the perimeter of the airport and held there until their owners returned.

Another successful scheme was the Legion's London Taxi School which opened its doors to ex-Servicemen in 1928. Many of them had spinal disabilities which meant standing up to work for long hours or lifting heavy boxes and other equipment was painful and difficult. The idea for the Taxi School came from a veteran of the Second Anglo-Afghan War of 1878–80, the First and Second Boer Wars and the First World War, Lieutenant General Sir Edward Bethune. He suggested that men who had learned to drive during the war could be trained to become London taxi drivers. Lord Nuffield supported the scheme by donating a taxi for training purposes.

From the outset the school was a success although it was the most expensive of all the employment support schemes. It cost the Legion £2,000 (£126,500) per driver with the remaining £12,000 (£760,000) being supplied by the Ministry of Labour. The training was arduous, taking at least 12 months and often longer. Students had to learn the Knowledge, the quickest route from any given point in the metropolis to another within a six-mile radius of Charing Cross. It is said that London's taxi drivers have a larger and more developed hippocampus than other people because of the extraordinary amount of knowledge they have to

Below, left: Recruits at the
Legion's Taxi School examine
a newly delivered taxi.

Below, right: The recruits
had to learn the Knowledge
as part of the taxi training.
It was done on bicycles in
all weathers.

keep in their heads in order to get from A to B without hesitation and while keeping up banter with their fare-paying customers.

Such was the success of the school that it continued after the Second World War, slowly at first because of petrol rationing, but by 1951 some 125 men were being trained annually. The head of the school was a former Scotland Yard inspector, George Stedman, who had worked as an examiner in the London Carriage Office, known by the trainee drivers as the Snake Pit. He was a warm-hearted man with a firm hand and an absolute belief in the value of sheer hard work to gain

the knowledge required. He explained the impact it had on the men under his eagle eye:

When the blokes get really involved in all this it changes them, they don't think about anything but the knowledge. They've got maps stuck round the walls of their rooms at home and they spend all evening calling over [reciting street names in a route]. They wake up in the middle of the night, they start thinking of a run and they can't go to sleep till they've got it. The other day one of the wives came in to see me. She said her husband was always out in the evening, she was

Printing road signs at Royal
British Legion Industries in
Aylesford, 1970s.

certain he'd got another woman. He was always coming in so tired, she said, just when she'd like a little cuddle. Well of course he hadn't got another woman, he was round with some of the other trainees, practicing his calling over. If you've got a lot of kids in a small flat you can't concentrate properly.

The outdoor training 'saw men going out day after day, week after week, on bicycle or on foot, notebooks in hand, noting routes and "points" where taxis are usually picked up', wrote Fred Marks in the January 1947 *Journal*. Marks had the distinction of completing the course in nine months – an all-time record. 'When at long last the Carriage Office is satisfied [with your knowledge] then comes your driving test – a stiff one. You are directed into a narrow back street and told to turn your cab around. A private motorist would do it in 20 movements, perhaps. You must do it in three.'

Men who went through the Taxi School knew the value of comradeship and some described it as like being back in the Army when mutual support was so valuable. Some joined because it was the best employment they could get given their disabilities; others wanted the freedom to be self-employed. By the time the Taxi School closed its doors in 1995 over 5,000 men had successfully passed the famous Knowledge and the stringent driving test to become a London cab driver. At one time in the 1950s just under a third of all the capital's taxi drivers had come through the Legion's school.

So strong was the bond between the drivers that in 1933 they formed their own branch of the Legion and began to organise children's parties and other charitable events. Today, any veteran can hail a Poppy Cab on his or her way to and from the Cenotaph and they will get the ride for free. The drivers of today are just as happy to help the veteran community as their forebears were after the two world wars.

Over time the Legion's responsibilities towards keeping men on the move changed. Part of the Legion's welfare focus today is on helping elderly and injured veterans to live independently, providing mobility kit, riser chairs and making adaptations to houses and flats to ensure they can have a life at home for as long as possible. Another part is dealing with younger ex-Service personnel who find the switch from life in the Armed Forces to civilian life challenging. Assisting with employment is a small but important part of what the Legion does. Small amounts of help to ex-Service personnel can be just as valuable today as they were 100 years ago.

Opposite: Tim Mackereth completed 22 years of Service, leaving the Army aged 40. He turned to the Legion for support starting up his own blacksmith business and 14 years on runs an award-winning company.

Below: Today the Legion offers advice on matters including debt, addiction, loneliness and care.

Chapter 5

——————————————

HANDS ACROSS
THE SEA

——————————————

HANDS ACROSS
THE SEA

At the heart of the Royal British Legion are people. It is an organisation that deals with individuals: returning Servicemen and women, their wives, husbands, widows, children and orphans. To the Legion everybody is an individual with a family story. And those individuals are spread all over the world.

THE BRANCHES AT HOME

In the early days, the best way to organise the help the Legion could offer was to set up local branches. The Legion, which had committed itself to ensuring that no one fell through its welfare net where at all possible, tried to encourage a countrywide network of branches to carry out this vital work. At the peak in the 1950s there were 4,750 branches throughout England, Wales and the island of Ireland. Today there are 2,500 branches, the same number as at the outset. The Legion divided England into ten areas and Wales into three. Some areas decided to delegate responsibilities to individual counties, but the key was to have a structure in place to ensure that help flowed efficiently and in the right direction.

It is important to remember that a great number of veterans from the First World War were in their twenties and thirties by the time the branches were

Above: Members of the LGBTQ+ and Allies Branch of the Royal British Legion, formed in 2019.

Opposite: The Riders Branch was formed in 2004. Members are seen at motorcycle events wearing the distinctive riders' badge. They became

synonymous with the repatriations of fallen Service personnel.

Overleaf: Royal British Legion branches around the UK.

set up. These were vibrant places in the community that provided entertainment and comradeship for members. Some had football or cricket teams while others had a bowling team and most played darts. Some of the women's branches had impressive athletes. There were inter-area competitions for all kinds of sports and annual competitions at national level. The Women's Section took part in athletic events and on 30 August 1922 Mary Lines set a new world record in London, running 880 yards (805 metres) in 2:26.6, beating the previous record, set ten days earlier in Paris, by almost 5 seconds. At that same Legion rally, held at Crystal Palace in the presence of the Prince of Wales, Gosforth Branch football team beat the Hackney Branch by six goals to nil.

In addition to town and village branches, a few were set up specifically to focus on one or another occupation and are not geographically based. These are known as National Branches and include Riders Branch (motorcyclists), the National Professionals Branch and LGBTQ+ and Allies Branch, which was formed in 2019, 19 years after the UK government lifted the ban on gay and bisexual people serving in the Armed Forces. Ann Miller-McCaffrey, who is currently serving in the Royal Navy, is a member of the branch along with her wife Emma Miller-McCaffrey. There is also the Y-Services (Garats HaY) Branch for former members of signals intelligence. The largest national branch is St James' Branch, which was formed in 1989 to allow individuals who either could not be or did not wish to be members of local branches. The membership now stands at 14,500 and operates as a virtual organisation with no premises of its own. As it is such a large branch with negligible running costs it has been able to make substantial donations to the Legion's welfare

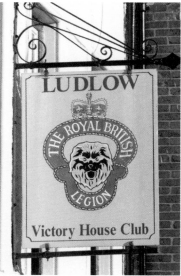

fund from the annual subscription fees. It continues to expand and is exploring opportunities for online membership and hopes to attract and retain more current Servicemen and women as members.

The branches continue to be the vital eyes and ears on the ground for the Legion's welfare programme and their role in Remembrance remains as important as ever.

PILGRIMAGES

Many branches undertook trips and made pilgrimages to France, Belgium and further afield to visit graves of men from their area who had not come home. The sense of belonging to a 'family' was important for the ex-Servicemen but also for their families. Anthony Brown, author of *Red for Remembrance*, wrote: 'Though the essential part of its work is to help the living, the Legion has never ceased to be aware of the nation's debt to those who died for it. In a sense, they are its deepest inspiration.' It was one of Earl Haig's early pledges, which was to ensure that the spirit of brotherhood and friendship that had been so evident on the battlefields be maintained in peacetime. Pilgrimages continue today and are important for those who go on them to visit the graves or memorials of family members, and also for those who organise them.

Some of the most moving pilgrimages were to the Dutch towns of Nijmegen and Arnhem. In September 1944 British Forces involved in Operation Market Garden attempted to take the bridge over the River Waal at Nijmegen but hasty reinforcement by the Germans thwarted the effort and many Allies died. The locals witnessed the battles and watched the British soldiers burying their dead. At first, they

Below, left: The Stone of Sacrifice at Jonkerbos War Cemetery in Nijmegen, Holland.

Below, right: Entrance to the South Africa (Delville Wood) National Memorial in the Somme.

Above: The Kohima Memorial, India, bears the epitaph:

When you go home
Tell them of us and say
For your tomorrow
We gave our today

spotted three or four graves; then the number rose to 20 and by the end of the first week there were 400 men buried in a makeshift cemetery. After the fighting moved on the villagers were left with the scars of war all over their landscape and a temporary burial ground with at least 17 unidentified burials. One of the local women said that she and her children would 'adopt' those boys and make them part of their family. Three months after the battle the villagers held a service of dedication at the cemetery, borrowing an altar from the church. They continued to lay flowers on the graves. 'That was really all we could do until the end of the war,' said one of the villagers years later. In the aftermath the Commonwealth War Graves Commission removed the bodies to other, larger cemeteries. Most of the dead were moved to a temporary cemetery created by No. 3 Casualty Clearing Station, in a wooded area known as Jonkers Bosch, from which it took its name. After the war, the permanent cemetery was established nearby. Jonkerbos War Cemetery contains 1,629 Commonwealth burials of the Second World War, 99 of them unidentified, and 13 war graves of other nationalities.

The people of Holland decided after the war that anyone coming from Britain or Allied countries to visit the graves of a family member would be a guest of the Dutch once on Dutch soil. People extended hospitality as generously as to a member of their own family. They took the visitors to the cemetery to help them find graves and then brought them back to their homes for bed and board. The costs for the visits were raised by 12,000 Dutch Poppy Collectors who collected money for the Netherlands War Graves Commission (NWGC) annually. When representatives of the Poppy Collectors came to London in June 1954 they were treated royally. On a visit to Windsor Castle their leader wanted to make a speech of thanks to their British hosts but the National Chairman, Captain S H Hampson, told him that it was the British Legion that owed a debt of thanks to the people of Holland and the NWGC. As he wrote in the *Journal*: 'Nowhere do the graves of Britain's war dead receive more devoted care than in the Netherlands. Each one has been adopted by a Dutch family who tend it regularly and keep in touch with the relatives.'

Over the course of their visit the British families were taken on excursions to the tulip fields, if the season was right, or to Amsterdam to see the canals. The Dutch hosts were christened The Goodhearts of Nijmegen by General Sir Brian Horrocks, who had been in command of XXX Corps (30 Corps) during the battle at Arnhem (Operation Market Garden) in September 1944. A Legion member who had made many visits to the area with grieving families explained what it meant to them:

After the initial shock of seeing a grave of a son or husband the tension can be almost unbearable. But then there is the church service the next day which all the relatives come to. In some way that's difficult to describe, this breaks the tension. After it the atmosphere changes – the tensions goes, people are ready to talk much more happily, exchange memories with their Dutch hosts.[11]

In October 1954 a Canadian, who had travelled 4,000 miles to see the grave of his son, was quoted in the *Journal*: 'I can go back content that his last resting place is being well cared for and that he lies among

kindly people. When I hear the stories of the starvation
and the humiliation which the Dutch suffered, I am
proud that I gave my son to help in their liberation.'

Pilgrimages organised by the Legion continue today
and although the numbers of mothers and widows
visiting graves are lower, they can still be deeply
moving occasions. In October 2009, there was a
pilgrimage to Kohima, in north-east India, where
British, Indian and Gurkha troops faced overwhelming
odds in repelling a Japanese invasion and were
engaged in one of the fiercest battles of the Second
World War. One of the pilgrims, Jim Gibson, was on a
mission to inter his aunt's ashes in the grave where her
husband was buried in 1944. Lance Sergeant Robert
Bell Hannay had been fighting with the 1st Queen's
Own Cameron Highlanders and in March 1944 he
and his regiment were dispatched as reinforcements
to relieve the besieged garrison at Kohima. He was

killed in action on 14 April. Ten days later his wife Ellen
received a brief note from the Infantry Records Office
in Perth from which she learned the dreadful news.

For the first weeks she was struck with grief
but then she heard of a two-year posting with the
Women's Voluntary Service in Southeast Asia.
She applied and was sent to Calcutta. Jim Gibson
wrote later: 'In her mind there undoubtedly lurked a
notion that it would be easier to get to Kohima from
anywhere in Southeast Asia rather than starting
from Glasgow.' With a great deal of assistance from
the British military she managed to visit the new
cemetery on the former battlefield of Garrison Hill
on 26 December 1945. She was the first widow to
visit the grave of her husband at that cemetery. Over
the next 55 years she went to Kohima eight times,
making the arduous journey by bus from Dimapur,
the final time being in 2000.

Ellen Hannay died in 2009 and Jim Gibson carried out her final wish. 'And so, on Friday 16 October 2009 and after much work establishing permissions, airline requirements and import regulations, I stood at Uncle Bob's grave in readiness for the short but very special task ahead.' Jim's aunt Ellen had told him about Mr Samuel Mezhur and his son Mr Atuo Angami, who were supervisors of the cemetery at Kohima. With the assistance of Mr Angami, and his son, Mr Sekhose, Jim Gibson laid his aunt's ashes to rest in her husband's grave. Peter Cleminson, the then National Chairman of the Legion, his wife Una, who is the current Chairman, and the National Standard Bearer, Royal British Legion, Nikki Archer-Waring, witnessed the moving ceremony.

He also placed the hat-badge that she had been wearing when she first visited Kohima Garrison Cemetery in 1945. When Peter Cleminson spoke the words of the Exhortation, he altered the last line to say: 'We will remember Ellen.' And the group responded: 'We will remember Ellen.' A week after he returned to Glasgow Jim was sitting at home remembering the lovely ceremony at Kohima and a thought sprang to his mind which remained with him for the rest of the day: 'Ellen would have loved that.'

Pilgrimages to battlefields and cemeteries on the Western Front and further afield were not just British affairs. Branches of the Legion from all over the world made efforts to bring veterans and family members to commemorate their fallen. In June 1934, 350 South African veterans, including a handful of widows of those who died in France, travelled 7,000 miles to the Somme by horse, ox-wagon, car, train and liner at their own expense. They stopped off in London to lay a wreath at the Grave of the Unknown Warrior in Westminster Abbey. They wrote in the *Journal* of their visit. 'We come not only to pay homage to the Dead, nor only to see again those spots like Delville Wood, where we lived and fought and died in an existence that was partly high adventure and mainly horrific nightmare. So we want to see what has happened to this England of ours as a result of all that.' They were received with warmth and a great show of ceremony in London, making their way from the Abbey to St James's Palace where they met the Prince of Wales who shook hands and had a word with each member of the party.

The following day the veterans were guests in the garden of Buckingham Palace and there was a closing dinner at South Africa House with dignitaries from the Legion, the Armed Forces and the government. The next day they travelled to Paris to kindle the flame at the Tomb of the Unknown Soldier beneath the Arc de Triomphe and then on to Delville Wood, where the 1st South African Infantry Brigade made its debut on the Western Front with disastrous casualties. It was an emotional time for the small number of the widows of the 2,536 men who were killed in the battle of Longueval Ridge and in Delville Wood itself. Many of them had never been to Europe before and had only heard about the Somme in letters from their late husbands.

The Legion has always understood the value of visits to the battlefields and cemeteries of both world wars. Over the course of the last 50 years it has organised major events to mark significant anniversaries, such as the 90th anniversary of the Great Pilgrimage of 1928, and the 75th anniversaries of D-Day in 2019 and of VE and VJ days in 2020. These will feature in the Conclusion of this book.

OVERSEAS BRANCHES

The Legion is the only military charity to have a worldwide system of branches and that is a unique and important feature of its existence. Currently it has 78 overseas branches but this figure changes as new branches are set up or old ones close. In the 1920s there were branches in every country from where Servicemen had come, offering a reminder of the great commitment made to Britain by the then Empire, colonies and dominions. Over 30 per cent of the men fighting for Britain were from today's Commonwealth and their governments supported the war effort financially as well as sending men and women.

Of the 1.1 million Servicemen who perished in the First World War, some 300,000 were from overseas. Their families' needs post-war were the same as those of the men who returned to Britain. There were branches in Tanganyika (Tanzania) and Kenya, Hong Kong and Gibraltar, Paris and Cologne by the end of 1921. Many are still active today, including Paris and Gibraltar. The *Journal* reported in October of that year that special dispensation had had to be given for the formation of a branch in a former enemy country. Colonel Edward Heath, the Legion's first General Secretary, had been with the British Army on the Rhine post-war and felt it was right to set up a branch of the Legion in Cologne.

Opposite: A driver stands beside a car decorated for Remembrance Day in Africa, c.1920s.

Top, right: Poppy Day in Ceylon (Sri Lanka), 1920s.

Right: Poppy Day in Kenya, c.1927.

THE CARIBBEAN CONTRIBUTION

At the outbreak of the Second World War British official policy stated that only 'British born men, of British born parents, of pure European descent' could become officers in any of His Majesty's Armed Forces. This ban was lifted on 19 October 1939 officially allowing British colonial subjects, including black candidates, to receive commissions as officers.

Thousands of men in the Caribbean signed up to help fight Britain's enemy, Nazi Germany. Mark Johnson wrote in his book *Caribbean Volunteers at War*: 'In a strange twist of fate, the free black grandchildren of the former slave populations of Europe's colonies had now come to help secure the release of Europe's new generation of white slaves from bondage. And they came of their own volition.'[12]

Right: Flight Lieutenant John Blair DFC trained as a navigator and survived a full tour of 30 bombing operations between December 1944 and May 1945.

Far right and opposite, top right: John Blair briefs for a Transport Command flight in the early 1960s; with his air crew in the same era.

Above: Flight Lieutenant Lincoln Lynch was an Air Gunner with 102 Sqn RAF. He was awarded the Distinguished Flying Medal (DFM) in September 1944 which cited his 'high standard of determination and devotion to duty'. He became a civil rights activist in 1960s United States.

In all, 15,000 West Indian men sailed with the British Merchant Navy and of those a third lost their lives at sea. The recruitment of 495 aircrew for the Royal Air Force was to see a similar proportion of casualties with 128 deaths. A further 6,000 men volunteered as ground crew and were trained at RAF Filey in Yorkshire. Caribbean people, including British-born Lilian Bader, the first black woman to serve in the regular British Armed Forces, worked in a technical capacity.

The men and women from the Caribbean were quickly seen to be equal to their British counterparts but this did not stop many of them being subjected to racist abuse. 'Billy' Strachan from Jamaica made his own way to Britain by ship when war broke out. He spoke of his experiences: 'When you arrived anywhere as the first black man you were treated like a teddy bear. You were loved and fêted … Two, they coped with … It was when three or more arrived that racism really got sharp.'[13] Undaunted, Strachan persisted and later flew 30 missions as a wireless operator. He then retrained as a bomber pilot and flew a further 15 missions over Europe.

ASTON KARL AIKEN

Aston Karl Aiken from Kingston, Jamaica, volunteered in 1941 at the age of 21, spending three years training in Canada then England flying Mosquitos. His brother, Roy Oswald Aiken, served as RAF ground crew, training in Yorkshire. In 1944 Aiken was promoted to Flying Officer and posted to 107 Squadron on 26 May. He and his pilot, Flying Officer Wilburn Macmilne Taylor from Canada, flew 28 missions between June and early August, including one mission in support of D-Day on the night of 5 June.

On 7 August they were among seven aircraft that attacked railway sidings in the Rouen area. They failed to return. There were rumours that their plane had hit a telegraph pole, but some in the squadron believed Taylor was a daredevil and flew lower than recommended and that their plane was destroyed by the fire on the burning train.

Aiken was 24 years old. He is buried at Connantre Communal Cemetery with his 29-year-old pilot. Aiken told his family on his last visit to them that he was not sure he would return, so when they heard he was missing they naturally feared the worst. When Taylor's mother heard that her son had been killed, she collapsed and died of a broken heart. Aiken's family were proud of his record and continue to wear poppies with pride on Remembrance Day. Aiken is commemorated, along with his fellow countrymen who fell in the First and Second World Wars, on the Jamaica War Memorial in National Heroes Park in Kingston, Jamaica.

COMMONWEALTH AND EUROPEAN ALLIES

It is an oft-repeated phrase that after the fall of France in June 1940 Britain stood alone against Nazi tyranny, and on the edge of Europe. Geographically speaking that is true, but it is not the case that the country was wholly alone. None did more in rushing to Britain's side than the volunteer forces who appeared from all corners of today's Commonwealth. This included 2.5 million men and women from undivided India, the largest volunteer army in the history of the world, while wealthier Commonwealth nations contributed not just armed forces but millions of pounds in cash aid and war materials. At the other extreme, villages as far afield as the Punjab and the Caribbean pooled their resources to purchase aircraft for the RAF. These were assigned to squadrons whose names paid tribute to their donors: Jamaica, Trinidad, Ceylon and Nigeria Squadrons to name just a few.

Polish and Czech troops and members of their air forces escaped to Britain in the summer of 1940 and pilots from both air forces were to fly with success in support of the RAF. The 145 pilots of the Polish Air Force who fought in the Battle of Britain, their flying skills honed during the invasion of Poland, were more effective than the less experienced British Commonwealth pilots. By the end of the war there were 19,400 Poles in the Polish Air Force in Britain and in the RAF. In addition, the Norwegian merchant fleet was put at Britain's disposal and sailed back and forth across the Atlantic, losing almost one-third of its fleet and men in the submarine-infested waters. Denmark was a government-in-exile in Britain and lent its substantial gold reserves to prop up the British war effort. A group that came in disarray but soon banded together to be a strong independent force were the men and women from France who escaped occupation and who, under General Charles de Gaulle, formed the Free French Army. Additionally, the British effort was aided by the highly efficient French Resistance, under the command of the Special Operations Executive (SOE) and directed by Jedburgh teams.

From 1940 a top-secret organisation called Special Operations Executive, known in wartime as 'Baker Street', began to train men and women typically from Nazi-occupied countries in the ungentlemanly art of guerrilla warfare, sabotage and radio communication. Theirs was among the most dangerous of roles as they were to be airdropped or flown into their own countries and encouraged to meet up with underground movements and carry out acts of sabotage and murder against the occupiers. More than 100 of those engaged in this work died at the hands of the Nazis, many of them in concentration camps.

On 15 October 2010 Stéphane Hessel, a 93-year-old former diplomat, stood up to make a speech at the unveiling of a plaque at Buchenwald concentration camp. It was to commemorate all the Free French who had been held there and executed before the camp's liberation by the Americans on 11 April 1945. Hessel was the last of the three men who survived to tell the tale of their persecution by the Nazis. The remaining men had been hanged. Hessel and two others had escaped by switching identities with three men who had died of typhus. He was recaptured and sent to Dora concentration camp but managed to escape a second time when he was being transferred to Bergen-Belsen in 1945. He fled to Hanover where he met the advancing US Army troops. Sixty-five years later he delivered the speech, switching fluently between

Above: Stéphane Hessel, SOE agent, Nazi concentration-camp survivor, diplomat and author.

IN MEMORY OF
THE ALLIED OFFICERS OF BLOCK 17
MURDERED HERE
SEPTEMBER 1944 - MARCH 1945

SPECIAL OPERATIONS EXECUTIVE

ALLARD, Lt E A L   LECCIA, Lt M
BARRETT, Flt Lt D J   MACALISTER, Capt J K
BENOIST, Capt R M C   MAYER, Lt J A
BOUGUENNEC, Lt J   MULSANT, Capt P L
DEFENDINI, Lt A B   PERTSCHUK, Lt M
DETAL, Lt J T J M   PICKERSGILL, Capt F H D
FRAGER, Maj H J F   RECHENMANN, Capt C T
GARRY, Lt E A H   SABOURIN, Lt R
GEELEN, Lt P A H   STEELE, Capt A
HUBBLE, Capt D E   WILKINSON, Capt G A

SECRET INTELLIGENCE SERVICE
KEUN, Capt G P G

And their colleagues who survived or who also died in this Camp

At the going down of the sun and in the morning
WE WILL REMEMBER THEM

Above: Memorial to the SOE men executed at Buchenwald concentration camp in 1944.

Opposite: Members of the Chinese Labour Corps in Egypt during the First World War.

French and English, after which he recited the names of all those who had died and were commemorated. He spoke without notes, a remarkable achievement for the ceremony's Guest of Honour, but then Stéphane Hessel was a remarkable man.

The idea for the memorial came from the Special Forces Club in London who contacted Robin Greenham of the Berlin Branch of the Legion. The event at Buchenwald included members of the Berlin Branch and their Standard Bearer. It was a small affair with just 60 attendees, but it was of huge significance to the relatives of the deceased SOE officers who attended the moving ceremony. They now have a permanent memorial to visit. This is one of the roles the Legion fulfils all over the world. It facilitates Acts of Remembrance and reconciliation, which bring together groups of people, whether former enemies or Allies.

BRANCHING OUT

In Germany there are 15 branches of the Legion spread all over the country. The only European nation that has more branches is Spain with 30, reflecting the large expatriate community in that country. There are a further 38 stand-alone branches as far afield as Fiji and the Falkland Islands. Hong Kong and China has an active branch, as do Thailand and Japan (Tokyo). Kenya is the only African nation to have its own branch of the Legion today but in the past there were branches from Egypt to South Africa. These had the same welfare commitments as their British counterparts and served the ex-Armed Forces community in a similar manner. In addition to the Legion there is also the Royal Commonwealth Ex-Services League (formerly the

BESL), which receives annual funding from the Legion, a founding member to which it is deeply committed. This organisation operates out of Haig House and has recently been working to increase support for Commonwealth veterans of the Second World War and their widows who live in extreme poverty.

The Legion has a vibrant branch in Kyrenia, Cyprus, which was founded in October 2011. It is the only branch in the Republic of Northern Cyprus and Turkey. Fifty years after the end of the Cyprus Emergency, hundreds of British veterans flew out to attend the unveiling of the memorial in the Old British Cemetery in Kyrenia honouring the 372 Servicemen who lost their lives in that four-year campaign between 1955 and 1959. It was the culmination of a 30-month project designed to ensure that those who died – most of them National Servicemen – should not be forgotten by the country to which they were never to return. The memorial has now become part of the island's Festival of Remembrance, which is held annually at the Old British Cemetery. The branch has a busy and varied calendar of events which raises funds to be used for the welfare cases that average about three per month. Kyrenia is a branch that is growing and will continue to encourage new and younger members to join.

The Portugal and Atlantic Islands Branch is the only one in the Legion family that covers an entire country and two islands. It was formed in July 1956, but a British Old Comrades Association had been active in Lisbon since 1920 largely thanks to the efforts of a British Army officer, Lieutenant Colonel Pope MC. The branch held services of Remembrance every year in Lisbon with the president of the Women's Section laying a wreath at the Cenotaph in Lisbon and another at the Combatants' League Monument of Alcobaça.

Right: Members of the Chinese Labour Corps in Boulogne, 1918. Over 100,000 Chinese worked with British and French Forces in the First World War.

The Old Comrades remained independent until the mid-1950s during the period when Legion branches were restricted to Britain and the Commonwealth but when this was relaxed a branch was formed. The branch continues to be active today and honours not only the British but also the Portuguese dead, and seven German airmen who were killed in the Second World War when attempting to land their aircraft on the Portuguese west coast. The annual Remembrance ceremony is attended by the German Consul, a naval officer from the German Embassy as well as the president of the local council and members of the

Portugal and Atlantic Islands Branch of the Legion. This Act of Remembrance is a reminder that the Legion respects the dead of all wars, whether friend or foe.

In Spain there is a focus on integration. The Coín Branch in the Costa del Sol encourages its members to get involved in the local Spanish community, to learn the language and to attend festivals. When the branch first suggested Spanish lessons, the local council was so positive about the idea that it ran a series of council-run classes, which were then promoted throughout the region. In this one simple way the branch has had the

effect of knitting together its members with the wider community. Like all branches, it has a strong focus on welfare and caring for those in need of assistance. While most of the attention is focused on the overseas branches' fundraising activities, Poppy Appeals and Remembrance services, it is this behind-the-scenes, everyday assistance that is such a vital part of the work.

The Hong Kong & China Branch had first been set up in 1921 to help the families of British ex-Servicemen who had returned to Hong Kong after the war and who had fallen on hard times. The branch was active in the early years, caring for the needs of families rendered destitute during the 1920s. The Hong Kong Cenotaph, a direct copy of the Lutyens' one in Whitehall, was unveiled in May 1923 and is located between Statute Square and City Hall with beautiful views over the harbour. Over the years the city has become more built up and it is no longer possible to see the water from the site, but the Cenotaph remains a constant reminder of the lives lost in both world wars and other conflicts.

The Hong Kong & China Branch closed when the Japanese invaded Hong Kong in December 1941, but was reopened in 1946 to care for the Chinese and British Servicemen and families who had suffered in the Far East during the Second World War. There were scant resources to hand then and there was no welfare system in Hong Kong, so the branch set about the task of raising and using money to help the bereaved, the wounded and sick, and, mostly, the destitute. Hong Kong still has a limited welfare system and those Chinese ex-Servicemen and their families who have welfare needs have the branch to turn to. So the work of the branch has not changed. In the 1970s Chinese characters were added to the Cenotaph to respect the lives lost during the invasion of the island by the Japanese:

英魂不朽 浩氣長存

which translates as 'May their martyred souls be immortal, and their noble spirits endure.'

Right: The Hong Kong Cenotaph is a replica of the Lutyens Cenotaph in Whitehall and was unveiled in 1923.

Far right: The Hong Kong Cenotaph today in its original position but with very different views.

The oldest and one of the most active branches is the Paris Branch. It was formally set up in June 1921 but its first meeting was held on 4 May when, according to its written history, 'a party of gentlemen, mostly belonging to the Veterans' Association then formed in Paris, met to consider the formation of the Paris Branch of the British Legion. They decided then and there to start the branch and it was in the following month of June that it fairly began to work.' They were fortunate to have high-powered support: Lord Hardinge of Penshurst and Marshal Foch agreed to be Honorary Presidents and Rear-Admiral Sir Edward Heaton-Ellis was elected Chairman. Lord Hardinge was the serving British Ambassador in Paris and had been Viceroy and Governor-General of India from 1910 to 1916. Sir Edward had a distinguished war record, commanding the Battlecruiser Squadron in HMS *Lion* and in August 1917 was appointed Naval Liaison Officer in Paris. Marshal Foch had served as the Supreme Allied Commander during the First World War. He accepted the German surrender on 11 November 1918 and believed that the Treaty of Versailles was too lenient on Germany. He said, as the treaty was being signed: 'This is not peace. It is an armistice for twenty years.' In that he turned out to be correct. Marshal Foch was always a great friend to the Legion. He had been made a Field Marshal of Great Britain in 1919 and made several visits to the UK up until his death in 1929.

The Paris Branch had a great deal of welfare work to do in the early days. Many Servicemen had married French women and when they found themselves in trouble during the Great Depression they turned to the Legion.

Opposite: Field Marshal Haig and Marshal Foch were both active on behalf of British Legion branches at home and abroad.

Below, left: Marshal Foch inspects Indian troops in France, 1927.

Below, centre: A recently refurbished advertisement for comforts offered to pilgrims by the Legion in Belgium.

Below, right: Haig House in Ypres was a hive of activity for pilgrims who wished to visit cemeteries on the Ypres Salient.

It was not just British men who married and settled in France after the war. One example of a man who was helped by the Paris Branch was an ex-junior officer of the Bombay Cavalry who had lost his right arm in action. After the war he had married a French woman and they had two children. With his war gratuity he had bought a small business in Amiens, but he ran up debts and was forced to sell the business. He went to Paris to look for work, but his savings were soon used up. The 1925 booklet about the history of the British Legion in Paris takes up the story: 'He very properly came to the Legion and it succeeded in finding work for him and fighting over his pension with the Indian Government until at last a satisfactory settlement was reached.'

Two important Legion events occur annually in Paris. One is the Service of Remembrance that first took place in Notre-Dame at 3pm on 11 November

1924. The Prince of Wales unveiled the British Commonwealth Memorial Plaque in the presence of the President of the French Republic, Gaston Doumergue, and Marshal Foch. With the exception of the four years of Nazi occupation during the Second World War the service has taken place annually, organised by the Legion with help from the British Embassy Defence Section. The service is open to British and Commonwealth nationals and anyone else who wants to take part. It is a most impressive ceremony and the Notre-Dame is always full. Since the terrible fire that destroyed most of its roof in April 2019 the Service of Remembrance has moved to the Cathédrale Saint-Louis des Invalides.

The second is the Pedal to Paris which started in 1995. The cycle ride is an inclusive event with keen amateurs as welcome as those with more experience.

The Legion organises every detail, including overnight accommodation, food and the transport of luggage and cycles back to the UK. It takes place annually and is a major fundraising opportunity. Over the years thousands of riders have taken part, cycling from London, through the Kent countryside with a stop at the Royal British Legion Village at Aylesford. From there to Dover and a ferry to Calais, where a Remembrance Service is held. From the coast the route takes them to Abbeville where, in 2019, riders joined in celebrations marking the 75th anniversary of the liberation of the town. From Abbeville the route steers the riders past the cemeteries marking the battlefields of the Somme, via Amiens and to Beauvais, a city damaged in both world wars. And finally, and triumphantly, to Paris, where they cycle as a peloton along the Avenue des Champs-Élysées, specially closed for the occasion, to the Arc de Triomphe. It is one of the special occasions, along with the Tour de France, that the Champs-Élysées is closed to traffic. On the 2019 ride Lieutenant General James Bashall CB CBE, the Legion's National President, had the honour of laying a wreath at the Tomb of the Unknown Soldier. He said later: 'It was a remarkable and moving occasion. The huge roundabout at the Arc de Triomphe had been closed and as I laid the wreath I had a great sense of how much the Legion and its observance of Remembrance means to people not just in Britain but all over the world.' [14]

The Ypres Branch had an extra responsibility over and above welfare and Remembrance. From the mid-1920s it offered families the opportunity to purchase a poppy wreath and have it placed on the grave of a man lost in the war. When the designs of wreaths available from the Poppy Factory had been finalised, a leaflet offering this service was produced and thousands of families took advantage of the scheme, happy in the knowledge that someone had visited their loved one's grave. Legion members continue to provide wreath-laying services for bereaved families to this day. Others wanted to visit the graves or memorials in person and branches would direct them to the Ypres team who could help them to find cemeteries and point them towards battlefields. They also offered help with practical information such as lodgings or eateries. The Ypres Branch was formed in 1925, two years before the Menin Gate Memorial was unveiled. It celebrated its 90th anniversary in 2015 and continues to be active in the town.

Right: Cyclists complete the Pedal to Paris ride at the Arc de Triomphe, September 2019.

BRANCHES TODAY

There can be no doubt that the branches were at the forefront of the welfare crises between the wars and after 1945. That they continue to have a role in looking after members of the Armed Forces community who need their assistance is a sign that the Legion is still an important part of the veterans' community. An initiative called Branch Community Support was launched in 2016. It is aimed at supporting the Armed Forces community in local areas, tapping into the invaluable resource of the eyes and ears of branch members. The support offered is simple, easily delivered by trained volunteers but invaluable to those who need it. The Telephone Buddies scheme, designed for people living alone and struggling to get out and socialise, proved especially important during the summer and winter of 2020 when the coronavirus pandemic left many, not just veterans, isolated and lonely. Home and hospital visiting is a popular initiative with volunteers offering comradeship to those who are unable, for whatever reason, to meet others face to face or who have no visitors.

Another key service in this offering is bereavement support. Branches can supply Legion representation and sometimes a Standard Bearer at a funeral. It often follows that branch members continue to visit the bereaved families after the funeral and this can be a consolation, especially if the death is untimely or a result of an accident or death in Service.

The Legion is always on the lookout for opportunities to raise awareness in communities of the services it can offer and is particularly good at identifying other bodies that can help if it cannot. An example was a case of an injured veteran who was struggling to make his rental payments. He contacted the Legion as a last resort, which was able to work with various authorities to secure him the pension and benefits that were due to him. When the arrears were paid the veteran was in receipt of a six-figure sum.

With a presence in almost every town in Great Britain and Northern Ireland, the Legion is well set to provide this kind of assistance. Although the Armed Forces community is not as large as it once was, the Legion still has responsibility for some 6.2 million serving and ex-Service personnel and their families in Britain and many thousands of others worldwide.

Chapter 6

_____

WORKING THROUGH OTHERS

_____

Above: The Duchess of York, later Queen Elizabeth The Queen Mother, with Princesses Elizabeth and Margaret at the annual sale of work by the Disabled Soldiers' Embroidery Society, London, 1933.

WORKING THROUGH OTHERS

Since the earliest days, the Legion has championed the causes of the returning ex-Servicemen and women, serving personnel, and their families. The campaign for better pensions for veterans, widows and the disabled occupied the minds of those concerned with the ex-Service community even before the Legion was set up. It has never wavered in its determination to see government held to account for its duty towards those who have served and been prepared to make the ultimate sacrifice. One example of the Legion's tenacity which had a beneficial outcome was the post-Second World War campaign on war pensions, resulting in the Pensions Appeal Tribunals Act of 1949. The National Executive calculated that it had cost £1,770 (£63,800) to run, had produced 2,800 press and news cuttings which had kept the Legion in the public eye throughout, and had realised an extra £1.2 million (£45 million) paid to pensioners annually.

Not all campaigns have such a good outcome, and many have been hard fought in the face of considerable lack of commitment by the government of the day. Lobbying for better pensions and disabled payments has been on the Legion's agenda since day one of its existence and it had many battles to persuade reluctant ministers of the importance of its message.

WAR PENSIONS

The War Pensions Act stipulated that a man had to prove that his disability or infirmity was a direct result of his war service. If this happened seven years after his Service had ended, he was no longer entitled to a review of his compensation. There were several conditions that only manifested themselves several years after the end of the war. Many succumbed to rheumatism as a result of life in the trenches, while men who had fought in campaigns further afield picked up intestinal infections that would gradually, over the course of years, have a severe impact on their long-term health.

One of the most distressing aspects of the seven-year rule was the situation faced by war widows. If her husband had died within seven years of the end of his Service, she was entitled to the full War Widow's Pension. If, however, he died after that, even if his death was directly attributable to his war wounds, the pension was reduced. This was so manifestly unfair

Right: A delegation from the British Legion at 10 Downing Street, December 1933.

that the Legion felt it needed to be dealt with. In a strongly worded article in the January 1923 edition of the *Journal*, entitled 'If only her husband had died a day sooner', A G Webb, head of the Legion's Pensions Department, pointed out the iniquity of the seven-year limit for widows:

> The Legion's view, which I have expressed over and over again in these pages, is that a widow should be entitled to a pension if her husband died of a disease, which had been recognised as attributable to or aggravated by Service, *irrespective of the date of death*. At present, if her husband dies one day after the seven years he leaves his wife pensionless. Picture the feelings of a mother watching by her invalid husband's bedside on the last day of the seventh year. Imagine the feelings of the dying man! It would be ridiculous – if it were not tragic.

He railed against the 'officialness of officials' and the Treasury who put 'parsimony before humanity' and expressed his anger that widows finding themselves in this position had to fall back on the Legion or accept Poor Law relief. Later that year the government agreed to consider applications on behalf of widows whose husbands had died after seven years and one day or more. Over the next eight years a few concessions were agreed by the government which meant that the Legion could appeal on behalf of more widows, but the seven-year rule remained rigidly in place. In 1931 Major Brunel Cohen, indefatigable as ever, introduced a Bill in Parliament to remove the limit altogether. Cohen pulled no punches. He told the Commons how appeals to the Ministry of Pensions were successful in 1 in 19 cases whereas appeals to the independent Appeals Court were successful in 1 in 4 cases.

He levelled a claim at the Minister of Pensions who, a few weeks previously, and before his appointment to the Ministry, had spoken up in favour of removing the time limit from the 1921 War Pensions Act. Cohen said: 'If the Minister held those views as a private Member, then it would say very little for public life if the fact of his going into office three weeks later altered them. I do not believe that the Minister has altered his views.'[15] The speech was well received and Cohen was praised by members on both sides of the House afterwards but soon after that the government was dissolved and a new Conservative government was elected. Cohen retired as an MP and the Legion lost its most energetic representative on pensions and disability in the House of Commons. Nevertheless, the point had been well made and although the seven-year rule was not abolished until 1943, sufficient concessions were made to have more or less the same effect.

Campaigning has been at the heart of the Legion's work since those early days and it continues in the 21st century. It is extraordinary that there are still issues that need the Legion's weight behind them to get the attention they deserve. Some campaigns take years of persuasion, discussion, negotiation and patience. Others are more immediately successful but all are put in front of the government of the day with the same amount of energy and well-researched explanation. As a result, the Legion has a success rate of over 90 per cent.

How campaigns come into being has varied over the years. Sometimes they are reactive, brought to light by a news story which they deem worthy of further investigation. Others come to attention as a result of welfare trends, while a third route might be from the membership, who have their ears to the ground. As the Legion is the dominant force in the military charities sector, a campaign might be recommended by a third party, such as happened when Blesma, The Limbless Veterans asked the Legion to look into compensation for lower-limb amputees. This was an example of the Legion using its influence to help another charity get an important issue dealt with at the highest level of government. In short, governments take the Legion seriously. As such, the Legion does not put forward campaigns that have little chance of success or for which there is no solution. It also knows that if there is no political will to deal with a certain problem, the campaign, however well organised, will fail.

HONOUR THE COVENANT

One of the most important campaigns the Legion has fought recently is Honour the Covenant. This was a campaign born out of a brutal time in the British Forces' history. For a decade at the beginning of this century the Forces, particularly the Army, had been at full stretch in Iraq and Afghanistan. The public's horror at the apparently never-ending flights of seriously injured military personnel and flag-draped coffins driven through Royal Wootton Bassett and, more recently, Brize Norton, resulted in the government agreeing to enshrine, in law, fair treatment and in certain cases, special measures to compensate for disadvantage arising from military service. The idea that the country owes its Armed Forces a debt when they put their lives on the line to protect the safety of the population is not new, but it was something that had been largely forgotten by a generation that had not known war. A professional military does not necessarily have the same goodwill as a volunteer or conscripted Army,

ARMED FORCES COVENANT

Navy or Royal Air Force, which was the case in both world wars. As a result, the public accords them that goodwill only if they believe it is deserved.

The Legion needed to remind the public and the government that a career in the Armed Forces differs from all others as Service personnel agree to sacrifice certain civilian freedoms and to follow orders. Sometimes those orders put them in harm's way in the defence of others. The Armed Forces Covenant, which currently has no force in law, is enshrined through convention, custom and contemporary application. It represents the nation's moral commitment to its Armed Forces. The Legion wanted to bring about change to ensure that Service personnel and their families get the support they deserve.

The campaign was launched in 2007, calling on the government to 'Honour the Covenant' by recognising the commitment and sacrifices by those who serve and their families, and ensuring just compensation and physical and mental health support were put in place. Initially the government was not keen to support it as they feared

it would leave them with a great deal of responsibility which, arguably, they already had. However, the campaign gained strong support inside and outside Parliament, and eventually the government moved to include the principles of the Covenant in the Armed Forces Act of 2011. It was a landmark piece of policy that has paved the way for other important campaigns that focus on fair treatment for the Armed Forces. It helped to persuade the government to acknowledge publicly that there are things particular to military life.

STOP THE SERVICE CHARGE

A campaign that received a lot of coverage was the question of visa fees for men and women from foreign and Commonwealth countries. Stop the Service Charge aims to remove the fees payable by Commonwealth Armed Forces personnel for the indefinite right to remain in Britain. Although these veterans have the right to remain once they have served in the British Armed Forces for four years, they must apply for this status, and the Home Office application process is expensive and complex. At the time of writing the visa application costs £2,389 per head, so that a family of four would have to find in the region of £10,000 to remain. This is a sum of money that few serving personnel know or have managed to set aside. Those who have been unable to afford the visa fees have been categorised as illegal immigrants, are unable to access free NHS treatment, and they face unemployment, homelessness and fear of deportation.

An added penalty of the process is that if the applicant makes just one mistake on the form, such as presenting a date in the American rather than British format, the appeal is cancelled and the application has

WE ARE THE LEGION

Opposite: A member of The
Queen's Guard was used to
illustrate the campaign to
Stop the Service Charge.

to be made and paid for all over again. This is not a situation unique to the Armed Forces, but it is out of tune with the government's drive for more overseas soldiers to bolster their recruitment efforts. The campaign has a blunt message:

> The UK relies on the bravery and sacrifice of members of the UK Armed Forces drawn from across the Commonwealth yet charges them thousands to continue to live here when they leave. This has to end. Exorbitant immigration fees are no way to say thank you for their Service, and risk pushing Commonwealth personnel into poverty just for wanting stability as they leave Service.

In 2018 the government declared its intention to recruit over 1,300 specialist and technical personnel a year from foreign and Commonwealth countries and it is hardly a good message that they will be hit with huge visa fees when they leave the Army, Navy or Royal Air Force but wish to stay in the country they have served. Currently there are 4,700 men and women serving with the British Armed Forces who will face this discrimination if they decide to apply to stay in the UK. It is a fight the Legion does not intend to give up on. The campaign was brought to the Legion's attention by its welfare teams who were concerned that families were spiralling into debt after leaving the Services as they could not access healthcare or civilian benefits.

COUNT THEM IN

A campaign that started in 2016 concluded in the spring of 2020. Called Count Them In, it had some of the most eye-catching images to push home its point. The Legion realised that there was no reliable and comprehensive data on which to plan services for the veterans' community. It became clear that the government was largely only aware of veterans who claimed pensions and compensation, not those who had served but not identified themselves to the authorities, for whatever reason, and were therefore invisible in official data. At the same time the 2011 census had included a question about identification which permitted thousands to identify as Jedi Knights but there was no question about military service. The Legion campaigned to get a new question onto the 2021 census that would allow for more accurate figures to be collated as to who has served in the Armed Forces. It is estimated that as many as 1 in 20 people in the UK have served at some stage.

The battle was long and hard fought. The Office for National Statistics (ONS), the body responsible for setting the census questions for England and Wales, and its fellow statistical agencies were initially resistant to the change arguing the data could perhaps be sourced elsewhere. The Legion's public affairs team worked with the governments of all four countries of the UK and eventually the statistics agencies did a U-turn and agreed to try out a sample question to see how robust it would be. The ONS accepted the Legion's argument in 2017. In September 2018 the National Records of Scotland recommended that the Scottish government include an Armed Forces question on the Scottish census. The Northern Ireland Statistics and Research Agency (NISRA) supported testing a question but in the end did not recommend its inclusion. Ultimately, however, the question was approved for the census across Great Britain, one of few questions to be added, a testament to the strength and effectiveness of the Legion's campaign and arguments.

Count Them In was a
successful campaign with
eye-catching imagery to
illustrate its point. In the
2021 census there will
be a new question on
military service.

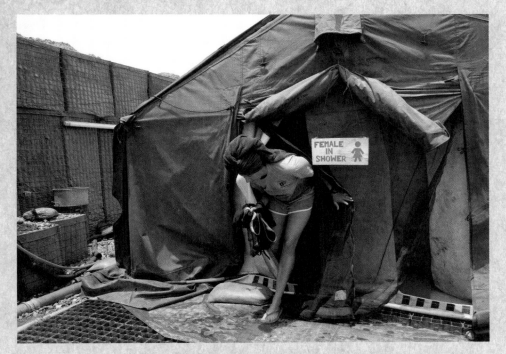

WOMEN IN AFGHANISTAN BY ALISON BASKERVILLE

In May 2012, the Legion sponsored the photojournalist Alison Baskerville to photograph the British Armed Forces in Afghanistan. She was embedded with them with the brief to develop a body of work exploring the changing roles of Servicewomen. She discovered the useful role women could play in compliance with local customs about gender separation, which was a surprise. The exhibition of her images was shown at gallery@oxo at Oxo Tower Wharf in London, and later travelled around the country. It showed intimate moments, as well as featuring women carrying out the same tasks as their male counterparts.

In 2019 she told *National Geographic*: 'As a young woman I made a choice to join the military. It felt very intentional at the time, and it's interesting to see how my views have changed following my time in Iraq and Afghanistan. It raised more questions than answers and set me on the path to exploring the very difficult relationships we have to those wearing a uniform. Working within this complexity is something I'm really interested in as a photographer and feels like a lifetime of work ahead of me.'

Chapter 7

————————

PEACE IN OUR TIME

————————

PEACE IN OUR TIME

'None can speak more eloquently for peace than those who have fought in war.' These are the words of Ralph Bunche, winner of the Nobel Prize for Peace in 1950, and is the motto of the World Veterans Federation, founded in the same year. It is not difficult to see that after two world wars in less than half a century those words would resonate with veterans of both conflicts.

Any returning Serviceman or woman will tell you that there is no glory in war. 'For ex-Service men know war at first hand. They have not merely read the bulletins; they have lived them. They have shuddered in the cold, they have sweated in the heat, they have felt the breath of the Angel of Death a hundred times. They have an exact appreciation of what war means; they have tasted it and found the flavour exceedingly bitter.' This description appeared in the *Journal* in June 1929 when the author, Hugo Bolton, was asked to reflect on the Whitsun bank holiday of 1914, 15 years earlier, when war had seemed an impossibility to the man on the street. Even after the assassination of Archduke Franz Ferdinand in Sarajevo men and women talked about war as if 'it was rather a picnic. Meanwhile the devil's brew was bubbling on a mighty cauldron, and for a generation which knew not war, there was being prepared a ghastly potion.' How, Bolton went on to ask his readers, could anyone wish for anything but the end to war as 'the final arbitrament between nations'?

The horrors of the First World War had produced an understandable loathing of armed conflict in both the Allied and Central Powers among veteran communities. Former foes all agreed that nothing as devastating should ever be allowed to happen again. In Britain, Legion members and other veterans believed they were uniquely placed to enforce this message and dissuade politicians from considering war as an option in settling international disputes. The Fédération Interalliée des Anciens Combattants (the inter-allied federation of ex-Servicemen), or FIDAC, had been founded by a Frenchman, Charles Bertrand, in late 1920. It included France, Great Britain, Belgium, the United States, Italy, Romania, Serbia and Czechoslovakia. One of its founding proclamations was that no former enemies could be admitted to the organisation.

At the FIDAC conference in 1922, members agreed to urge their governments back home 'to entirely disarm and disband land, sea and air forces and destroy the implements of warfare'.[16] Given the turbulent history of the 20th century it might seem naive that the organisations within FIDAC really believed they had the power to stop another war, but feelings ran high and it is hard not to admire their optimism that they could prevail. Two years later Sir Ian Hamilton, a veteran of the South African Wars and

the First World War, proposed at conference that the ban on former enemies joining FIDAC should be lifted. It was highly contentious. The French and Belgian organisations were firmly against it. When Germany was admitted to the League of Nations in 1926, Colonel Crosfield, who was at that time President of FIDAC, persuaded a reluctant conference to hold a meeting with ex-enemies in 1927.

Over the next few years and into the early 1930s FIDAC watched in dismay as the League of Nations, set up in 1919 for the purpose of maintaining peace, failed to stop the rearmament of nations. It was in a hopeless position with Germany, Japan, the United States and Russia wholly against any form of restriction on their military growth. The Legion kept up its pressure on the League of Nations, with which it had close relations, but the truth was that the European political landscape was changing.

PEACE MISSIONS OF THE 1930S

The Legion understood the benefits of meeting with former enemy ex-Service organisations and had been encouraging branches to contact their equivalents in Germany. There then came an episode in the Legion's history that has often been taken out of the context of the time and used to show how unsuspecting the Legion could be when dealing in the field of international politics. However, taken in context it is more comprehensible. Following all the informal contacts with German ex-Service organisations, the Legion received an invitation from Joachim von Ribbentrop, Hitler's unofficial ambassador in Britain, for a delegation to visit his country in the summer of 1935.

Colonel Crosfield consulted Anthony Eden, then Lord Privy Seal, and neither saw any problem with the Legion accepting. What no one could have known was how quickly and dangerously they would become associated with the German propaganda machine. The invitation was announced at the annual conference in June with the visit planned for the following month. One party would go to Austria and Hungary, the other to Germany. Conference approved the idea of the visits and it was then that the Legion's Patron, HRH The Prince of Wales, who had previously been informed of developments, stepped up onto the platform. His visit was not announced in advance. The delegates in the Queen's Hall were delighted when they saw who was walking onto the stage and greeted him with tumultuous applause. He finished his speech with the following:

There is one point which your President, when I was speaking to him the other day, brought up, and which also commended itself to me, and that is that

a deputation might go, or a visit may be paid by, representative members of the Legion to Germany at some future time. I feel that there could be no more suitable body or organization of men to stretch forth the hand of friendship to the Germans than we ex-Servicemen, who fought them in the Great War, and have now forgotten all about that.

The press reporters suddenly had a major story. 'Hand of friendship to the Germans' was the headline and it was flashed around the world within minutes, telegrams falling onto editors' desks in every country of the Empire and beyond.

The King was dismayed at what he saw as his son meddling in international political affairs and reprimanded him, but the Berlin correspondent of *The Times* wrote of the delight at the Prince's speech. He described how welcome the delegation would be in Germany and quoted Ribbentrop as saying: 'I am certain that the spirit which prevails in most ex-Servicemen's organizations in the various countries will prove a great support to the various governments in their endeavour definitely to establish peace and cooperation in Europe.'

There was opposition to the visit from politicians in Britain who feared it would be seen as a diplomatic mission backed by the government. Aneurin Bevan MP, representing Ebbw Vale, asked the Secretary of State for Foreign Affairs, Sir Samuel Hoare, in the House of Commons whether the government was aware of the planned visit and whether they sanctioned it. Hoare replied that they had indeed heard about it but that it was strictly an ex-Services matter and not an official diplomatic delegation.

In June the Vice Chairman of the Legion, Colonel Ashwanden, and Major Brunel Cohen went to Vienna,

which had been the capital of the Austro-Hungarian Empire allied with Germany in the First World War. After the war the Empire was dissolved and Vienna became the capital of Austria. There the British delegation were received by the Austrian Chancellor who spoke of the need 'of educating the youth to the horrors and dangers of war'. They met with Austrian veterans' organisations, all of which supported the Legion's gesture of establishing contact with former enemies. From Vienna they travelled down the Danube river through Hungary to Budapest, where they were met on the quayside by a guard of honour and an enthusiastic reception. The friendliness with which the ex-Servicemen greeted them was heart-warming and the delegation returned to London with messages of friendship and gratitude for the visit. The *Journal* reported how the Hungarians had insisted on paying all their hotel bills, taxes and for the odd meal too. Major Cohen concluded that the Hungarian ex-Service organisation was non-political and much like the Legion, the only difference being that their members always wore uniform.

The visit to Germany by Major Francis Fetherston-Godley, the National Chairman, Colonel Crosfield, a former National Chairman who spoke fluent German, and others was a much more high-profile event.

From the minute they set foot in Berlin in mid-July they were in the spotlight. The Germans had whipped up a storm of enthusiasm and when the British delegation was driven to the official reception, they saw thousands of Germans packed onto the streets, cheering and saluting them. Everywhere they went, whether to war cemeteries or a reception at Ribbentrop's house in the Berlin suburbs, they were saluted by enthusiastic crowds several deep along the routes.

The delegation met with German war veterans and were surprised into an unscheduled visit to the Reich Chancellery where they met Adolf Hitler himself. The six British men spent an hour and a half in the gardens with the German Chancellor exchanging war stories. Hitler liked nothing more than to reminisce about the war with veterans, it would appear. He told them that 'in the interests of peace he attached a special value to collaboration between soldiers who had fought in the last war'.[17]

Joseph Goebbels, the Reich Minister of Propaganda, had his efficient bureau working at full stretch. A photographer and film crew ensured that all aspects of the visit, and especially the meeting with the Führer, were well documented. The Berlin correspondent of *The Times* followed the delegation throughout. In Munich he reported on Major Fetherston-Godley laying a wreath of poppies at the Munich War Memorial. He added: 'According to the official programme published in the Nazi Press, this ceremony was to have been immediately followed by the laying of an identical wreath on the tablet erected in the Feldherrnhalle to the memory of the Nazi insurgents who were killed in the abortive *Putsch* against the Bavarian Government in 1923.' This was too much for the British. They had not been consulted and Fetherston-Godley refused on the grounds that it would be incompatible with their strictly non-political character and the nature of their visit to Germany.

The delegation left Germany convinced that Hitler did not want to go to war. It was the message Hitler wanted to convey but it was duplicitous. He had been building up Germany's armed forces for the previous two years and he had used the British visit to his own ends. In the light of what happened over the next

Opposite: Members of the British Legion delegation greet German disabled veterans, known then as 'Frontsoldaten'.

Below, left to right: The British Legion delegation to Germany were presented with a photograph album recording their visit to Berlin, Munich and Cologne in 1935. The citation translates: 'May our two peoples understand each other in the future as Tommy and Fritz do twenty years after the end of the war!'

Opposite, left: Mr Clive, the Legion's Standard Bearer, at a parade in Berlin, July 1935.

Opposite, top right: Members of the Hitler Youth lay flowers on the graves of British soldiers buried in Berlin South-Western Cemetery.

Opposite, below right: Captain Hawes (left) and Major Fetherston-Godley visit British graves in Hamburg cemetery.

four years it is easy to point a finger at the Legion dignitaries and condemn them as naive to have been taken in by their hosts. Yet, as others have argued, who would not have gone all out for peace just 20 years after the outbreak of such a devastating conflict that had cost so many lives and damaged even more forever? At the time of the visit the First World War was as near in memory as 9/11 is today.

At the time there was a lot of anger expressed both in the Jewish press and in branches of the Legion which had a strong Jewish element. The chaplain of the Maccabean Branch, the Reverend Michael Adler,

Zur Erinnerung an den
Besuch der Vertreter der
BRITISH LEGION
IN DEUTSCHLAND
« Mögen unsere beiden Völker in Zukunft sich
so verstehen, wie das Tommy und Fritz zwanzig
Jahre nach dem Kriegsende tun! »
BERLIN AM 15. JULI 1935

He reminded readers that over 12,000 German Jews had died fighting for Germany in the First World War.

Fetherston-Godley wrote in the August 1935 *Journal* of his disappointment that some newspapers had misconstrued the purpose of the Legion's visit to Germany. 'There was no political basis in it. Our object was to meet ex-enemy and ex-Service men whatever their nationality and thought. Whatever good it may do is in the hands of the future.'

GERMAN VETERANS VISIT BRITAIN

The German visit of 1935 was just one of a series of exchanges between British and German veterans' organisations. Already members of the Brighton Branch had been to Cologne in return for a party of ex-Servicemen from that city visiting them to find the grave of a German prisoner of war. In January 1936 there was a visit by a German ex-Service organisation to collect the standard of the Schwerfen Company of the Prussian Guards. It had been captured at St Quentin in September 1918 by the Shropshire Light Infantry. Swansea Branch organised the exchange with support from the National Executive and the visit was reported in the February 1936 *Journal*. The standard was handed over in a tense and dramatic silence. Then General von Muller spoke with emotion and unmistakeable sincerity. He said that 'he hoped that a better friendship among the three nations would spring from this beginning of a new connection between ex-Service men of England, France and Germany; a real friendship would mean peace forever'. He promised that on his return to Germany he would emphasise the real and sincere friendship with which his delegation had been received. Soldiers' promises

Above: The Legion delegation is welcomed in Berlin on the first leg of their week-long tour of Germany, 1935.

who had been the senior Jewish Chaplain with the British Forces in France and had been awarded the Distinguished Service Order, expressed his views in a letter to the *Journal*:

> The Jewish ex-Service man who did his duty in the War is none the less a patriotic Englishman because he strongly protests against the medieval intolerance meted out to the Jews in Germany. We Jews earnestly hope that the authorities of the Legion will make perfectly plain to the ex-soldiers of Germany that, whilst justice and liberty are denied to the Jews of their country, the Legion must strongly disapprove of this policy.[18]

Below, left: A medium struck
to commemorate the British
Legion delegation's visit to
Germany in 1935.

Below, centre: German
ex-Servicemen lay a wreath
on their visit to Brighton
in 1935.

Below, right: German war
veterans and members of
the British Legion at the
Cenotaph in Whitehall, 1937.

were kept, he said. He drank to friendship; to the branch that had made the present event possible; to the prosperity of Wales and England.

The Germans sent a telegram from the SS *Bremen*, 'Leaving England we want to tell you how happy we have felt amongst you. Many thanks for your hospitality. Our desire is to do our best for the sake of a friendly understanding between our countries.' Despite this warm note and his toasts in Swansea, von Muller went on to lead the 16th Panzer Division and was later convicted as a war criminal in the Soviet Union.

In May 1938 a delegation of 800 German ex-Servicemen arrived in London. The visit was not written up in the *Journal* and the only reference to it was one photograph of the principal people meeting at Victoria Station. The Germans had requested permission to march past the Cenotaph in Whitehall as a mark of respect to the dead of the Empire. This would have been unthinkable given

the political situation in Germany, so a compromise was achieved. The parade was staged behind closed doors at the Royal Hospital Chelsea. What a contrast were the marching German veterans in their navy-blue suits and caps to the scarlet-clad Chelsea Pensioners standing by.

Then came the Munich crisis of September 1938 when Czechoslovakia was thrown to the wolves in an attempt to appease Hitler and avoid war. Having occupied the Rhineland and annexed Austria, Hitler now set his sights on the Sudetenland, formerly part of the Austro-Hungarian Empire and by then part of Czechoslovakia. He argued that the area should be returned to Germany as the majority of the population were ethnic Germans. The British government intervened and suggested the matter should be voted on in a plebiscite. Hitler grudgingly agreed and accepted up to 10,000 members of the

British Legion to oversee this. Although men were gathered and expected to sail on 8 October events sped ahead of plans and on 30 September 1938 Hitler and Italian dictator Benito Mussolini signed the Munich Agreement which permitted the annexation of the Sudetenland. The other two signatories were British Prime Minister Neville Chamberlain, and French Prime Minister Édouard Daladier.

Put in context, the Legion's visit to Germany in 1935 was simply part of the bigger picture of the desire for peace at all costs and its attempts at reaching out to veterans across the divide. The reason it has been flagged up as such an important issue, and possibly a faux pas, in the Legion's history is because of the Prince's speech and Goebbels' ruthlessly efficient propaganda machine that turned a peace delegation into a major media circus.

This marked the end of the Legion's attempts to conduct diplomacy in pursuit of peace, but it did not stop visits and exchanges between former enemies. Soon after the Second World War, reconciliation visits were organised between the Legion and German ex-Servicemen's organisations. But these were low-profile events without fanfare. Groups met on the Normandy beaches as early as 1952 and individual families had exchange holidays in Britain and Germany to heal the scars of the second war between their nations in a quarter of a century. Fewer people in today's Britain are closely associated with men and women directly affected by their Service. The Legion is involved in teaching programmes in schools that encourage discussion around the two world wars. Children have the potential to help broaden the spread of the Legion's message to communities that have hitherto felt that Remembrance did not involve them.

DEFENDING THE REALM FROM HOME

At the 1939 Annual Conference the Chairman, Major Fetherston-Godley, stood up and told the delegates that although the Legion had campaigned vigorously for peace for almost 20 years, it would be resolute in the face of another war. The July *Journal* quoted his words: 'Make no mistake about this. If our country is attacked, we are going to defend it to the last. If our liberties are threatened, we are going to fight for them; if our friends are menaced, we are going to stand by them.' This was greeted with cheers of approval. The Legion offered its service to the government which, it claimed, asked them to set up a national defence corps of up to 25,000 men. This was to become the Home Guard and had at full strength 1.5 million volunteers of whom a sizeable number were ex-Servicemen. In 1940 Anthony Eden MP stood up in the House of Commons and made a statement distancing himself from this claim, stating emphatically that the British Legion had no formal role in setting up the force and that this was entirely the responsibility of the Territorial Army. However, the Legion was involved in recruiting and training. In October 1940 the *Journal* reported: 'In many parts of the country the Home Guard units are composed almost entirely of Legionaries, and in numerous other districts where non-Legionaries preponderate, sections, platoons, companies and battalions have been raised largely as a result of local Legion cooperation with the TA Association.' There was a regular feature on the Home Guard in the *Journal* wartime issues entitled 'Home Guard Notes and News', including cartoons and a whole page in November 1940 devoted to the carrier pigeon section. The feature continued to appear until the Home Guard was disbanded in December 1944.

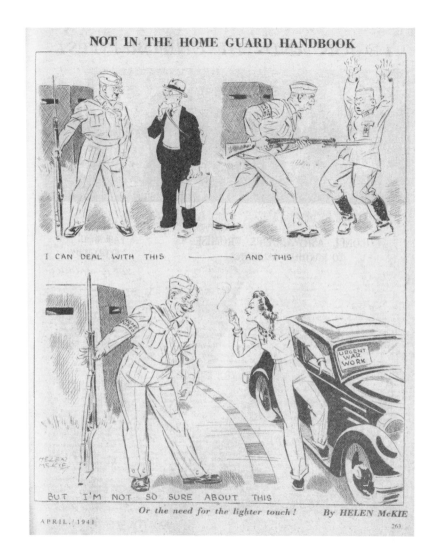

Below, left: Colonel Crosfield (right) greeted on Vimy Ridge by Lord Byng, the Mayor of Vimy, on the Great Pilgrimage, 1928.

Below, right: Peace protesters at the Greenham Common Women's Peace Camp, 1982. They were against the British government's decision to allow US cruise missiles to be stored there.

Opposite, left: Young and old protesters at Greenham Common in 1981.

Opposite, right: A Green Peace protester.

In June 1940, with the retreat from Dunkirk complete and the tragedy of the fall of France, the message in that month's *Journal* was defiant: 'Today the sons of Legionnaires are fighting to defeat the blood-lust of a criminal maniac, who straddles impudently across Europe as a menace to civilisation.' There was never any doubt expressed in the *Journal* but that the Allies would defeat Nazi Germany. As early as August that year the Legion was publishing plans for the post-war world. It predicted unemployment and urged the government to consider a major road-building scheme and to clear the slums of the inner cities, which it described as a blot on civilisation. The committee set up to oversee this was chaired by the indefatigable Fred Lister with Colonel Crosfield, equally tireless, as his Vice Chairman. They took their conclusions and recommendations to Ernest Bevin in 1941, who Churchill had put in charge of demobilisation that year, and continued to lobby the government on the welfare of returning men.

THE POPPY AND THE PEACE MOVEMENT

During the 1960s and 1970s the Legion struggled to make its voice heard among the angry anti-war protests that caused so much furore among the younger generation. They saw the Legionnaires with their smart blazers and standards, marching on Remembrance Sunday, as a symbol of the glorification of war, not as the promoter of peace which has always been the Legion's stand. The red poppy fuelled their anger and they responded by wearing white poppies as a symbol of peace. It led to a period of introspection for the Legion as it considered how to appeal to a generation who had never known war and saw the Legion's members as old fogies who liked to reminisce about their glorious battles. Britain was going through another period of severe economic pain with industrial action and strikes an almost everyday feature of life. The country was by now known as the sick man of Europe. There was high unemployment and inflation,

Right and below: Operation Banner in Northern Ireland was the longest British military campaign in history, running for 30 years from 1969, involving 300,000 members of the Armed Forces, and now constitutes the largest body of British veterans. There were children in the region who grew up with the Troubles as the only life they knew.

Opposite: Women's peace movement at Greenham Common, 1982. The protest turned into a blockade and the camp was finally disbanded in 2000.

unrest on the streets of many towns and cities, and racism was running rife. It was a difficult time and the Legion suffered as much as other organisations from the political, economic and social fallout.

Today the Legion remains as devoted to the idea of peace as it was between the two world wars but rather than involving itself actively in peace initiatives it helps to facilitate them for others. One of the ways it has done this is to provide a physical space for Acts of Remembrance and reconciliation at the National Memorial Arboretum in Staffordshire.

On 10 November 2000 the Secretary of State for Defence, the Right Honourable Geoff Hoon MP, announced, in reply to a question from fellow Labour member Vernon Coaker MP, that there would be a new memorial created to commemorate members of the Armed Forces who had died since the Second World War. This was the culmination of a series of debates about how best to respect the memory of the thousands of men and women who had died on active Service in the years after 1945. Hoon told the House of Commons that the memorial would be erected in London.

The idea was greeted with dismay by Commander David Childs CBE, a former naval commander, who since the early 1990s had been working on the creation of the National Memorial Arboretum on a site close to Burton upon Trent in the Midlands. By 2000 it was up and running as a going concern with thousands of trees planted and dedicated to organisations, both military and civilian, and it was beginning to receive a healthy flow of visitors. At this stage, the Arboretum was an independent body without any formal association with the Legion. However, the Director of Corporate Affairs at the Legion, Charles Lewis, was enthusiastic about the whole undertaking. He and David Childs shared a desire to reinstate the Two Minute Silence annually on Armistice Day at 11am, which had fallen out of use after the Second World War. In October and November 1995 a PR team, hired by the Legion, campaigned to raise the public's awareness of the Two Minute Silence and to create the opportunity to remember. This high-profile campaign successfully enlisted the support of the *Sun* and the

Opposite: The Armed Forces Memorial at the National Memorial Arboretum in Staffordshire commemorates over 16,000 men and women who have died in the service of this country since the end of the Second World War.

Left: Replica of one of two stained-glass windows made by Lt Cdr Upton RNVR, who was imprisoned in Java, 1942–5. Note the Churchillian lion smoking a cigar on the left.

Below: The Far Eastern Prisoners of War building was opened in 2005.

Daily Mirror. Polling after Remembrance Sunday that year showed that over 94 per cent of people aged between 16 and 24 wanted to have the Two Minute Silence reinstated at 11am on 11 November the following year and beyond.

The Women's Section of the Legion was involved in the Remembrance Sunday services held at the Arboretum from the outset and the local branch regularly lent its hall for events. However, it was not until 2004 that the Legion formally took the Arboretum into its fold. Since then it has flourished. Annual visitor numbers jumped from 50,000 to 300,000 after the unveiling of the Armed Forces Memorial in 2007.

David Childs felt passionately that it would be a mistake to build the Armed Forces Memorial in London and he began to campaign energetically to get the Secretary of State to change his mind. His arguments were convincing. In the first place there was ample space at the Arboretum for a substantial

memorial and that would be hard to find in London. Secondly, there was the question of cost: the land at the Arboretum was leased at a rent of £1 a year for 999 years so there would be no need to purchase land. Thirdly, a new memorial in London might detract from the Cenotaph for Remembrance Sunday. There was also the question of access. The Arboretum lies at the centre of the country with excellent road connections via the M1, M6 and other major routes. There was plenty of parking for visitors and the Arboretum was already dedicated to Remembrance. The final argument was that they could organise educational visits any day of the year. To the great satisfaction of the Board of Trustees and the Friends of the Arboretum they won the argument. In 2002 Geoff Hoon announced to the House of Commons: 'I am delighted to be able to confirm that the Armed Forces Memorial will be sited at the National Memorial Arboretum in Staffordshire.'

GREEN SHOOTS

The idea for a National Memorial Arboretum had come to David Childs not long after the end of the Cold War. He wrote of how the two world wars and the tail end of a violent century awakened in him an overwhelming awareness of the importance of Remembrance.

> Yet, out of these troubled times was born a generation most of whom lived their lives if not in total peace, certainly in freedom. But it was freedom bought at a great price ... we are in debt to those who were prepared to put their lives at risk so that we might be free, and we who owe the most need to remember the most, for the debt itself is unpayable. [19]

As a naval commander one of his tasks was to visit the Supreme Allied Commander Atlantic at its HQ in Norfolk, Virginia. On one visit he went to the Arlington Military Cemetery and then to the National Arboretum in Washington DC. In the middle of the night he woke up and realised that he could combine the two and develop a National Memorial Arboretum. On the flight home he read a piece in the *Daily Telegraph* about plans to plant a national forest in the counties of Leicestershire, Derbyshire and Staffordshire 'to help cover up and heal the scars of centuries of mining and other mineral extraction ... It seemed obvious that this was where any National Memorial Arboretum should be.' [20] The most supportive person in the early days was Group Captain Leonard Cheshire VC OM DSO & Two Bars DFC, Britain's most highly decorated pilot from the Second World War. He encouraged Childs to pursue his ambitious idea. Leonard Cheshire died in 1992 but his widow, Margaret Susan Cheshire, Baroness Ryder of Warsaw,

Lady Cheshire CMG OBE, who had served with the SOE as a volunteer during the war, continued to be involved with the fledgling Arboretum up to her death at the age of 76 in 2000.

It was one thing to come up with an ambitious idea but quite another to find the land, funding and expertise to develop something completely new. Childs was fortunate that key people were keen on the idea. Lichfield District Council expressed their support, as did the head of the National Forest, Susan Bell. Her father had been killed in Korea when she was still a child and she saw immediately what Childs was trying to achieve. The final stroke of luck came in the form of the land which was owned by Redland Aggregates and the experienced Restoration Manager, Ron Foster, was behind the scheme from the beginning. With all that expertise and enthusiasm, plus a board of trustees who had considerable influence, and a Friends group of local volunteers who would turn out to be the lifeblood of the whole project, David Childs' enterprise was in good shape. He admitted later that the expertise of the various official bodies was 'important for they would be dealing, in me, with someone who had no experience of estate management, planning, fundraising or planting; indeed, for most of my career close contact with a tree would have meant something had gone seriously wrong with my navigation.' [21]

Planned to be a project for the new millennium, the Arboretum was initially funded by the government. Its brief was to act as a centre of commemoration for the nation. Glades of trees would be planted to mark Remembrance for individual regiments, Armed Forces charities, the police, the fire brigades, war widows and many more besides. During the late 1990s there were many setbacks and tribulations. Saplings died

Opposite: An explosion of coloured paper marks the close of the Thank You Youth Festival at the National Memorial Arboretum in 2018.

Left: A bench plaque commemorates the golden wedding of Thomas and Mary Higgs. Thomas Higgs's ashes are buried under the foundations of the Polish Memorial.

in great numbers, the ground flooded in winter and in summer the earth baked hard. But there were also minor triumphs and major successes. Aided by money from the National Lottery, the trustees commissioned a visitor centre and chapel to be built. Small donations from members of the public often came with touching messages, such as one elderly lady who wrote: 'I would like a tree planted in memory of Flying Officer Ian Sutherland who died over Germany in 1940. He was the only man that I ever could have married and so I remain, yours sincerely, Miss —.'

The construction of the buildings and the planting of trees took years. In all that time the group of Friends of the Arboretum worked tirelessly and with great determination to make the dream a reality. They became a family and from the earliest days they treasured the stories that visitors and donors told them. Every tree has a reason for being there and behind every plaque there is a real human story of love or loss or simple Remembrance. Sue Elliott, a former WRNS (Women's Royal Naval Service) and an early member of the Friends, spoke of the happiness and delight visitors felt and continue to feel when they visit. It is not a place of sombre sadness but of joyful Remembrance and reflection. The largest number of visitors to the Arboretum are children, which is just as David Childs envisaged it 30 years ago.

One of the most beautiful glades was created in 2007 to mark the golden wedding of the Queen and the Duke of Edinburgh, and all couples who had married in 1947. The trees all have a golden theme in their bark or leaves. These include Golden Ash, Sorbus of various varieties and Malus Golden Hornet. In 1999 a circle of 10,000 daffodils was planted by Brownies and Girl Guides from Staffordshire. When the girls returned the following spring to admire the daffodils in flower, they were excited to see the result of their work. Some of them told the volunteers they could remember which ones they had planted.

There are amusing stories that come out of visits to the Arboretum and these are cherished by the Friends

Above: The Polish Memorial is one of the largest at the Arboretum and commemorates the Polish contribution in the Second World War. The associated organisations are the Polish Ex-Combatants Association, the Association of Polish Knights of the Sovereign and Military Order of Malta, the Polish Air Force Charitable Trust and the Polish Underground Movement.

who acted as volunteer guides in the early days. Guardsman Thomas Higgs and his wife, Mary, were a local couple celebrating their golden wedding. They bought a bench which was placed in the Golden Grove to commemorate the event. Sadly, Thomas died not long afterwards and Mary asked whether the casket containing his ashes could be buried under the bench. At that time this was something the Arboretum could offer; the practice stopped in the early years of this century. A few years after Thomas's death there was a plan to move the bench and replace it with an enormous bronze memorial to the Polish Servicemen and women. Sue Elliott was tasked with writing to Mary to ask her if she wanted the casket with her husband's ashes back so she could bury it elsewhere. The widow wrote back immediately: 'Oh no, leave them there. Thomas would be tickled pink to think he was so close to the Polish Memorial as he had fought alongside the Poles up the length of Italy during the Second World War.' The casket is now 20 feet below the ground, under the enormous foundations that were constructed to take the weight of the sculpture. The memorial bench with the plaque commemorating their golden wedding is close to the memorial.

By the time the Legion took over the running of the Arboretum in 2004 most of the early problems with tree planting and drainage had been sorted out. Work on finding an architect and artist for the Armed Forces Memorial was underway as well. However, it was not an entirely straightforward handover. For one, David Childs was concerned about the civilian memorials among the hundreds of Armed Forces dedications. There were memorials to the police, for example, and that might have been a stumbling block for the Legion but in fact it proved not to be the case. The Legion also discovered some outstanding legal issues with contracts and other paperwork problems but after three years of negotiating all was sorted out.

The Legion has a light touch at the Arboretum, preferring to let the organisation in Staffordshire make the running on outreach projects, educational tours and exhibition planning. It kept in place the key staff members and volunteers, whom the regular visitors recognised, so the change of ownership was seamless as far as they were concerned. What the Legion brought to the table was its organisational skill, its ability to think big and the financial backing to support projects for which the Arboretum previously had had to fundraise on an individual basis.

When the Armed Forces Memorial was unveiled in 2007 by Her Majesty The Queen it put the National Memorial Arboretum right at the heart of Remembrance – year-round, not just on Remembrance Sunday. The Armed Forces will be at the memorial in decades to come and the Legion will be there to support their Remembrance, as it has supported ex-Service personnel and veterans for 100 years at the Cenotaph.

The walls of the Armed Forces Memorial have the names of the dead inscribed on them, arranged by date and then alphabetical order. There are no ranks here. In death these men and women are treated as equals. Soberingly, there is space for another 15,000 names, reminding the visitor that there will be deaths among the Armed Forces from conflict or terrorism in the future.

The atmosphere within the memorial is one of peace and reverence. The great circular walls cut visitors off from the outside world leaving only the sky above them and the memorial around them. The quietness is sometimes overpowering and the

Opposite: An event held at the National Memorial Arboretum on 7 July 2017 celebrated the role of women at war over 100 years. Over 1,000 people took part in the commemorations.

208   WE ARE THE LEGION

THE ARMED FORCES MEMORIAL

The Armed Forces Memorial is the largest memorial on the site. It is the creation of the architect Liam O'Connor, with sculptures by the Gloucestershire-based artist, Ian Rank-Broadley. O'Connor's design won the competition that had been held to find the most appropriate monument to honour the 16,000 members of the Armed Forces who had died on active Service since 1945. What swayed the judging panel was the fact that through a slit in the wall of the great building the sun would shine on the altar stone at 11am on 11 November. It seemed a fitting tribute looking back to the traditions of Neolithic burial sites around Britain.

The enormous memorial is a tumulus that stands out from the main Arboretum on a hill and gives uninterrupted views over the site and the Staffordshire countryside beyond. Built of Portland stone, the building comprises two massive circular walls on which are inscribed some of the names of the fallen. Within the circle stand two rectangular walls against which Rank-Broadley's more-than-life-size sculptures are set to theatrical and poignant effect; one a stretcher-bearer party and the other a woman and man in uniform handling the naked body of a dead man. On their left is a man pointing to the partly opened door through which the light will shine onto the altar on Armistice Day.

whole creation has the same immense authority as the Menin Gate Memorial in Ypres or the Singapore Memorial further afield. Rank-Broadley's sculptures are expressive and moving. He succeeds in creating a sense of movement, tension, emotion and extraordinary pathos.

The most recent addition to the Arboretum is the Remembrance Glade which was unveiled in September 2020. The glade provides a space for reflection, which is evoked through symbolic forms, features and plants. The curved-oak gateways, representing strength and continuity, provide an entrance into an inner sanctum where a perfect circle of white-stemmed Himalayan birches create a sense of harmony and unity. The mirror reflects truth and brings light. It is a space for quiet contemplation of service and sacrifice, or simply somewhere for visitors to reflect on what Remembrance means to them.

Through the Arboretum the Legion continues to deliver the message that David Childs had wanted to convey, and others embraced so quickly. In search of mutual understanding it facilitates reconciliation events for those who stretch out the hand of peace across the divide between former enemies. Its vision is to be the nation's year-round place for Remembrance, a world-class inspirational setting free to all.

Right and opposite: The Remembrance Glade was unveiled in September 2020.

PEACE IN OUR TIME

Chapter 8

CREATING BETTER FUTURES

CREATING BETTER FUTURES

'When I get home, I'm writing a book called *How Five Days Changed My Life*.' That was a comment on an evaluation form submitted after a course at the Battle Back Centre at Lilleshall near Telford in September 2019. Another, from November 2018, started: 'I'm at peace with myself. Not so very long ago I was ready to walk down a live train track.'

When we see serving soldiers and smartly turned-out veterans, we see what we want to see: highly disciplined, well-dressed women and men in command of themselves and their work. Pride in what they do is evident in their manner, confidence in their colleagues in the way they speak about one another, dedication to duty is written all over their tattoos. But what happens when things go wrong? Who picks up the pieces after a young man has lost both his legs, or a young woman is blinded for life? And what about the veterans who are haunted by flashbacks and nightmares? This is the side of being in the military, on the front line, at war, that the public seldom sees or even contemplates. However, it is one of the areas of most importance to the Legion and it is as vital today as it was in 1921 when over 1.75 million men returned from the battlefields with some form of physical or mental disability.

The Legion's vision statement is that it is committed 'to bring together the nation, communities and

individuals to create better futures for our Armed Forces and their families'. Nowhere is this more evident than with the Legion's work providing hope for the future for those members of the Armed Forces wounded or injured in conflict.

THE BATTLE BACK CENTRE

The Battle Back Centre is another jewel in the crown of the Royal British Legion but, unlike the National Memorial Arboretum, it operates privately, away from the public gaze. But it certainly does not act quietly. It came into existence because of the recent operations in Iraq and Afghanistan and as a result of improvements in the treatment of severely injured soldiers. From 2003 to 2014 the military was engaged in back-to-back combat operations. The casualty figures for Iraq were 179 killed and up to 5,800 injured.

For Afghanistan there were 456 military deaths and 7,300 treated for battlefield injuries. In all, 21,000 men and women were discharged from the services for medical reasons.

When a soldier suffers what is described as a major blast injury, meaning loss of limbs and major internal injuries, the Medical Emergency Response Team, operating in a helicopter, will attempt to reach that soldier in ten minutes. This is known as 'Platinum' with life-saving first aid being provided by combat medics and colleagues. Advanced first aid provided within one hour is referred to as the Golden Hour. In earlier times that man or woman would almost certainly have died. With advances in battlefield medicine, such as haemostatic agents and applications, the team would attempt to get the injured person to a hospital in, say, Helmand, within

an hour. Following further treatment or definitive surgery their condition would be stabilised to the point where they could be transported back to Britain to the Queen Elizabeth Hospital Birmingham for further clinical treatment. Once their condition improved sufficiently, they would then commence the rehabilitation phase at Headley Court in Surrey. This has now been replaced by a new rehab facility, the Defence and National Rehabilitation Centre at Stanford Hall, a Grade II listed 18th-century country house in Nottinghamshire. It includes a £5 million complex trauma gymnasium gifted to the centre by the Legion.

In the First and Second World Wars that time to hospital in Britain would have been measured in days, if not weeks. The speed of repatriation often presents problems for those who are seriously wounded. One minute they might be lying on the ground, covered in blood, sand and other debris, and the next, in their experience, they are lying in

Opposite and right: Lilleshall Hall (opposite) is the Duke of Sutherland's 19th-century home and shooting lodge. It was gifted to the nation by South Africa in 1949 and now hosts one of three National Sports Centres. Within its grounds is the Royal British Legion's Battle Back Centre (right).

Right: Wheelchair volleyball
is the first physical activity
undertaken on a one-week
Battle Back course.

a hospital bed in Britain surrounded by bright lights
and teams of clinicians whose only concern is to
make them better. Sometimes the shock of such
immediate treatment takes time to assimilate and it
can leave the Serviceman or woman with a feeling
of dislocation. Recovery can often take months and
although the medical treatment is outstanding and
the physiotherapy for those who need it life-changing,
there is still the matter of starting again in the civilian
world. This is often where some of the greatest
problems lie.

Over the decade since the Battle Back Centre opened,
the number of men and women who are amputees
has dropped from almost 70 per cent per course to
virtually zero. Amputees and those with major injuries
are now the exception to the rule. Significantly, those
suffering from mental health issues has gone up from
just 5 per cent in 2012 to 50 per cent in 2017.

In 2009, Leeds Beckett University collaborated with
the Royal British Legion to provide additional recovery
support for wounded, injured and sick (WIS) Armed

Forces personnel. Both organisations recognised that
the Ministry of Defence now had a greater number of
individuals requiring help with both physical injuries
and mental ill-health. The Battle Back Centre was set
up to be part of the recovery pathway for WIS, where
adventurous training and sport is offered. It is run by
Leeds Beckett University, which supplies the trained
coaches and research staff who attend each course,
and is wholly funded by the Legion.

The Centre is situated at the Lilleshall National
Sports Centre near Telford. It has access to top-class
facilities on the Sport England-owned site, and it is well
situated in the centre of the country with good road
and rail networks. There are three levels of programme
available that have been designed by experts at Leeds
Beckett. Level 1 is a one-week residential multi-activity
course that the Centre runs 24 weeks in the year. Level
2 is a one-week specialised course of which there are
currently ten a year. The third level is expeditions, the
most recent being Ecuador and the Himalayas.

Just under half of the coaches at the centre are
ex-military and the aim of the courses is to help the
long-term WIS to build confidence for their futures
and to focus on what they can do rather than what
they cannot. The courses have been honed over the
last decade by the research team at Leeds Beckett
to produce the best possible outcome for the
Battlebackers, as they are known. Researchers from
Leeds Beckett survey the participants on arrival and
departure, then one and two weeks later, and then
after 3, 6 and 12 months, to assess the long-term
impact of the course. Their research consistently points
to an increased sense of autonomy, competence,
relatedness and improved mental well-being in those
who take part in the surveys, which is over 95 per cent.

Left and top: Cooperation and technical competence are both important aspects of building trust with climbing partners.

Above: Archery is one of the sports on offer at Battle Back.

Above and right: It has long been recognised by the Ministry of Defence that adventurous training has a major role to play in rehabilitation.

COURSE STRUCTURE

The Battle Back courses are carefully structured to ensure parity between the participants. One of the Battle Back course directors is Richard Lake-Bullen. He spent 24 years in the Royal Marines from 1970, serving all over the world, including stints in Northern Ireland, where he saw the impact of the Troubles close up. On retirement, after a spell working with business leaders, he took up the offer of work as a coach at the Battle Back Centre, joining in 2012, shortly after the pilot scheme had been a convincing success. He said:

> Coming into this was a massive eye opener. Dealing with mental health and serious injuries is a completely different world to what I was used to. Mental health is much more difficult to deal with because it is a hidden enemy. There are so many variants of PTSD [post-traumatic stress disorder] and there is no one overall solution. All we can do is to try and help them to learn to help themselves.[22]

He explained how the atmosphere at the Battle Back Centre has to be completely unthreatening. He emphasises right from the get-go that there is to be no judgement of others and respect is vital. The other thing he repeats is the millimetre challenge. The best way to get back on track is to take tiny steps and to build on them. 'I wish the participants could see the effect we have on them,' says Christopher Joynson, the head of the Battle Back Centre. 'It is so wonderful to see the difference between Monday and Friday.'

Joynson has been in charge of the Centre from the outset. He served in the Infantry in the Staffordshire Regiment and is proud that members of his family

have served with that regiment since 1907. His Service ran from 1976 to 2012 when he retired as a lieutenant colonel. His last posting was in an Army Recovery role in the West Midlands and on his retirement he joined the Legion to set up and run the Battle Back Centre. He said it is one of the most rewarding jobs there can be. There is a further reason why he is so committed to the Centre. His grandfather served in the First World War with the South Staffordshire Regiment and later with the Royal Flying Corps, the predecessor to the Royal Air Force, flying in Farman Experimental 2b aircraft – often thought to be the most dangerous of roles with average life expectancy and time in the air less than 22 minutes. When he returned to Britain after the war, he was suffering from shell shock and had great difficulty readjusting. Joynson says: 'Today he would have been diagnosed with PTSD and accorded degrees of sympathy and respect that did not exist then. He never recovered to lead a full life after the war and died in his early forties. Supporting those with PTSD is particularly important to me.'[23]

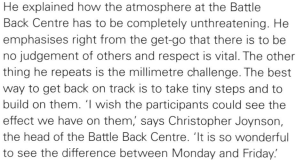

Right: Participants also take part in group sessions looking at behaviour, anger management and problem solving.

ON TOP OF THE WORLD

In November 2018 Joynson was joint leader of a team that went to the Himalayas to climb Mera Peak, a mountain in Nepal standing at just under 6,500 metres (21,300 feet). The aim was to reach the summit on 11 November, to mark the 100th anniversary of the end of the First World War. In the group were ten veterans, three serving men and women and five Battle Back Centre staff.

The 13 members of the team had been chosen from more than 30 applicants and represented a diverse mix from all three Services: male, female, serving and veterans, ages ranging from mid-20s to mid-60s, and including one serving and one former Royal Navy doctor. Expedition leaders Dave Bunting and Christopher Joynson and four of the team summitted on the morning of 11 November 2018, as planned. The day was brilliantly clear with bright-blue skies and almost wind-still. The view from the summit was of white peaks all around and the unmistakable shape of Mount Everest on the horizon, its tell-tale plume of snow visible in the distance. They gathered for the team photograph, grinning with delight and pride in their achievement and unfurled a banner to mark a literal high point in the Legion's national Thank You movement to mark 100 years since the end of the First World War.

The following day Richard Lake-Bullen, Christopher Kay and a fifth Battlebacker stood on the peak and surveyed the world below. Of those Battlebackers who did not summit, all made it to Khare camp at the edge of the Mera glacier, which lies above 5,000 metres. For a group with no previous mountaineering experience, this was a major achievement. The Himalayan expedition was judged by all to have been a success

on so many levels. Joynson knows that adventures like this can help to change lives, but he also acknowledges there are some people whose needs are so complex it is not possible to find a cure, just a way to live with their troubles. The expedition underlined how exercise and maintaining a basic standard of personal fitness can play an important role in optimising the quality of life that veterans can enjoy.

POST-FIRST WORLD WAR

The well-being of ex-Servicemen and women has always been of primary concern to the Legion. From the earliest months of the First World War the number of men returning with horrific, life-changing injuries as well as mental trauma was high. At first, hospitals were overwhelmed by the nature of the wounds they had to treat, including tens of thousands of men with faces damaged beyond recognition and others with one or two limbs missing. Over the course of the war the treatment of the wounded developed and improved dramatically. Men who would have died in field hospitals

Opposite: The Battle Back team on the summit of Mera Peak, 11 November 2018.

Below, right: Gardening at Preston Hall village, 1930s.

in 1915 stood a chance of getting back to Britain for treatment by 1917.

As well as the wounded, men were returning from the trenches with diseases, such as tuberculosis (TB). TB was a long-term problem and one that concerned the Legion in its early days when over 55,000 men had returned from the war suffering from the disease, of whom 18,000 had died by 1922. In the early 20th century TB was one of the UK's most serious and urgent health issues. In the previous century one in every four deaths was from TB and the figures were only a little lower going into the First World War. A highly infectious disease of the lungs, in the main, it spreads rapidly in insanitary, cramped conditions. The trenches had proved to be an ideal spreading ground and many sufferers returned to similarly unsanitary conditions at home. The poorer areas of big towns and cities were slums that became TB hotspots. There was little effective treatment until well after the Second World War and the best way to manage infection was to isolate the sufferers and quarantine them in hospitals, sanatoria and, later, villages.

PRESTON HALL AND THE LEGION VILLAGE

The Legion decided that the best way to help the sufferers would be to create a village, based on the model of the Cambridgeshire Tuberculosis Colony, set up by Dr Pendrill Varrier-Jones in 1916 and expanded two years later when it moved to the Papworth Hall estate. In 1925 the Legion acquired Preston Hall near Maidstone in Kent. At the time it was a large Victorian manor house surrounded by 200 acres of farmland and was being used as a model farm for disabled ex-Servicemen. Taking over both the hospital and the

training scheme, the Legion immediately began to plan an ambitious programme.

Dr Varrier-Jones helped to set up and run the hospital for its first year and his experience was invaluable. He recommended the Assistant Matron from Papworth, Miss Elizabeth Lee, to be Matron at Preston Hall. It could not have been a better choice. Miss Lee had served in Salonica as a Yeoman nurse and had been awarded the ARRC (Associate of the Royal Red Cross) for her work. She was renowned for her gentleness and it was said that she never took a day off in the 20 years she worked there. In her obituary, published in the *Journal* in October 1945, Colonel Crosfield described her as the Mother of Preston Hall and praised her abilities in nursing and her understanding of TB, which was so valuable to the Legion. The hospital expanded and the 198 patients who were already there grew in number to almost 500 by 1928. The Legion had succeeded in removing infected men and women from among the general population and offered hope and a new life to the sufferers. In those days fresh air was considered essential and outside wards were a common feature at TB hospitals and

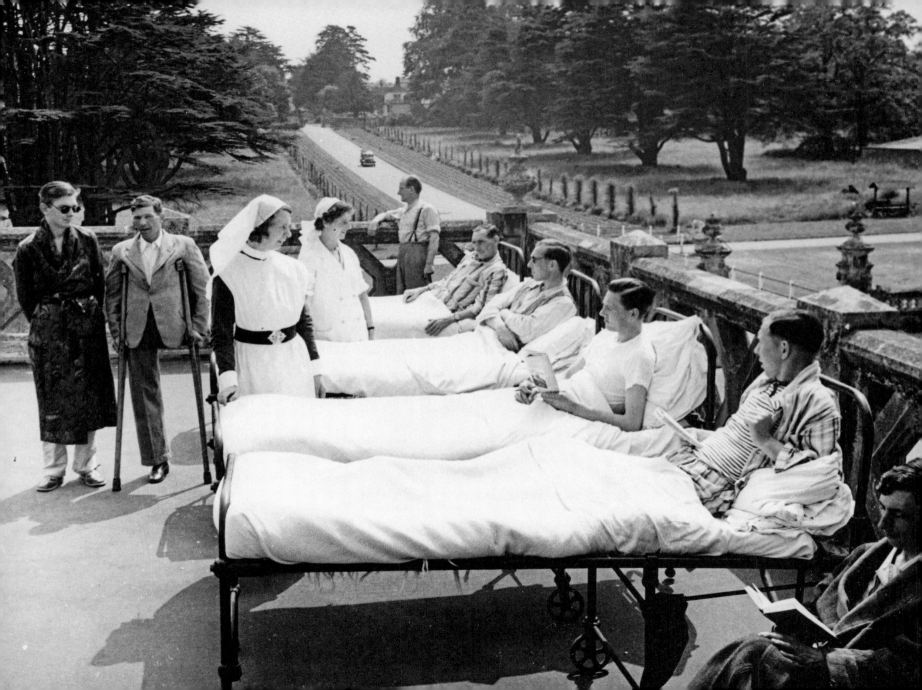

sanatoria. Preston Hall was no exception. The medical team also made sure to keep up with the most modern treatments, one of which was medical and surgical collapse therapy which had to be undertaken in an operating theatre. In simplest terms, a man's infected lung would be collapsed to rest it and allow the lesions to heal. It was a technique that had been used in the mid-19th century and continued to be used until after the Second World War.

The Legion acquired Douglas House in Bournemouth which became the seaside TB ward. It also took over a 150-bed sanatorium at Nayland in Suffolk for the treatment of ex-Servicewomen suffering from the disease. By the outbreak of the Second World War, Preston Hall had 150 sanatorium beds. A further 360 beds were created to form a General Hospital that was administered by the Legion throughout the war. In 1944 the *Journal* claimed that the Legion, with its three TB institutions, was the largest single unit in Europe fighting the disease.

Not all men suffering from TB needed permanent hospital care. Some were able to work, albeit in more limited occupations than others. The creation of a village in which they and their families could be housed developed into a community with a church, restaurant, village shop and workshops, all built by the Legion, and more than 120 houses. Preston Hall became the British Legion Village and signs on the A20 announced its existence.

Once the Welfare State was born in 1948, Preston Hall passed into the hands of the local health service, though the Legion still had a representative on the board. Responsibility for dealing with the disabled of the Second World War fell to the fledgling National Health Service. Thanks to the strides made in the

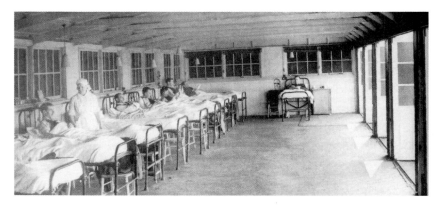

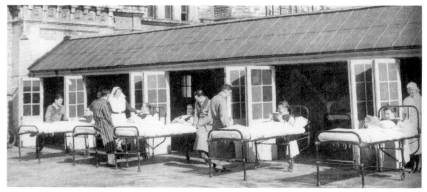

Opposite: Treatment for TB in the first half of the 20th century involved outdoor wards as seen here at Preston Hall.

Above: By 1928 there were some 500 patients being treated for TB at Preston Hall.

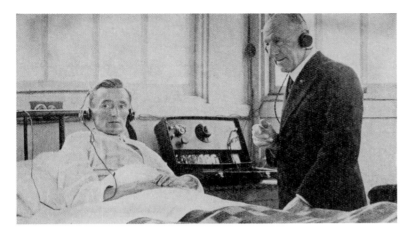

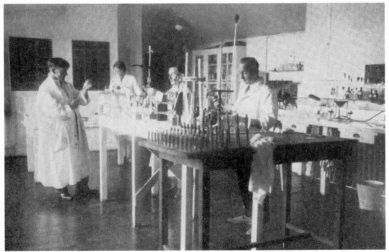

Top: Tuning in with a patient at Preston Hall.

Above: The laboratory at Preston Hall was modern and well run by the Legion. It was taken over by the NHS in 1948.

treatment of serious physical injuries after the First World War, there was more knowledge about how to treat cases of amputees, burn victims and those otherwise physically incapacitated by war. There had also been improvements in the understanding of shell shock, recognised in the late 1940s as a serious condition. Once again, the Legion was on the case. Of the 130,000 men thought to be suffering from what is now called post-traumatic stress disorder, the Legion reckoned only one in four was getting the medical treatment needed. As the October 1945 *Journal* put it: 'To give them a pension if they haven't one is no cure. If medical treatment is necessary it must be made readily available to all, and it must carry with it no real or imagined stigma. And wife and family must be adequately cared for.'

The Legion always believed that if a disabled man were able to work it would help him to maintain his sense of self-worth. The idea of providing sheltered employment for the men who could work grew into a reality. Royal British Legion Industries (RBLI) at the Village at Preston Hall employed a workforce of disabled men who were involved in making heated pads and blankets for the hospital, as well as in printing, pallet manufacture, injection moulding, light metal fabrication and the production of traffic signs. The workforce continued to grow and by 1966, with cases of TB falling sharply, the Legion took on men with other disabilities and output continued. By the late 1970s, half a century on from its early beginnings, RBLI's annual sales stood at about £1 million, which almost covered the cost of giving the men employment.

Below, left: Disabled
ex-Servicemen on an outing
on the River Thames in
September 1931, organised
by the Not Forgotten
Association, which works
with the Legion.

Below, right: Nurses from
the National Spinal Injuries
Unit with Professor Ludwig
Guttmann, who ran the
unit from 1944 until his
retirement in 1967.

POST-SECOND WORLD WAR

The post-Second World War rehabilitation strategy for the Legion was focused on helping men and women with physical injuries regain some control over their lives and have something to look forward to. In the 1920s and 1930s the expectation for people with a serious spinal injury was that they would spend the rest of their lives on their back. During the Second World War the Ministry of Pensions set up a hospital at Stoke Mandeville to deal with cases of spinal injuries. Until 1944 the treatment was poorly coordinated, and many sufferers died of infected sores or urinary tract infections. Enter Professor Ludwig Guttmann, a German Jewish neurosurgeon considered to be the leading specialist in neurosurgery of his generation. He escaped from Germany just before the outbreak of war and was given assistance to get to Oxford where he and his family lodged with the Master of Balliol College. He worked at St Hugh's College on research but in 1943 he was asked to set up a new unit to treat spinal injuries. In February 1944 he was appointed medical director of the National Spinal Injuries Centre (NSIC).

Guttmann ran the unit with singular authority and took full responsibility for all aspects of patient care, overseeing everything from catheterisation to physiotherapy and sport. He refused to accept that an ex-Serviceman with spinal injuries could not take part in life in the future. In the main these were young

Opposite: Wheelchair archery was the first sport introduced by Guttmann at the Stoke Mandeville Games in 1948. These female archers were competing in 1950.

Below: The aim of the Stoke Mandeville Games was to 'unite paralysed men and women from all parts of the world'.

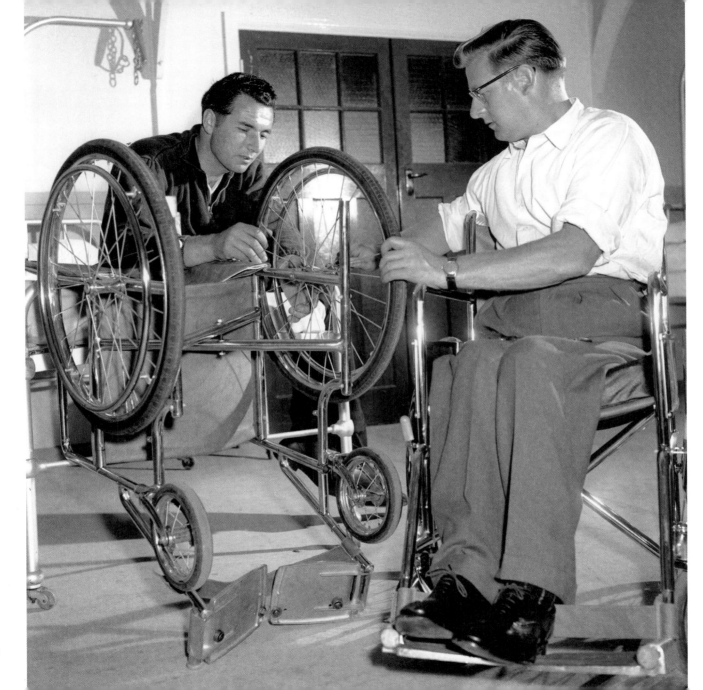

men and women in their twenties and, unlike their counterparts from the First World War, they were not destined to die of infections due to poor-quality nursing and a lack of understanding about possible treatments. The British Legion was entirely onside with Guttmann's approach and sponsored or 'adopted' several men at the NSIC, helping with wheelchair ball sports and trips to football matches.

As the patients made progress, Guttmann moved from recreational to competitive sports. On the day of the opening of the London Olympic Games in 1948, he organised the Stoke Mandeville Games where 16 patients, including women, took part in an archery competition. Four years later Dutch ex-Servicemen joined the games and with that the seeds of the Paralympic Games were sown. They took place every four years and in 1960 were held in Rome where they were given their official title. The first Paralympics held in cooperation with the Olympic and Paralympic Organizing Committees, and using shared venues, were held in Seoul, South Korea, in 1988. Over 100,000 people attended the opening ceremonies, which featured skydivers, thousands of children, and 700 wheelchair dancers. In 2014, Prince Harry, Duke of Sussex, unveiled the Invictus Games in Queen Elizabeth Olympic Park in London, 66 years after Guttmann's first Stoke Mandeville Games and 54 years after the Paralympics were officially founded. At the inaugural Games more than 400 competitors from 13 nations took part.

Opposite: Mending wheelchairs was a year-round necessity, not just for the Games.

Right: Wheelchair javelin thrower training at Stoke Mandeville, ahead of the 1964 Tokyo Paralympics.

THE INVICTUS GAMES

The Invictus Games were inspired by the Warrior Games set up in the United States to allow injured ex-Service personnel to compete in a wide range of sports. Prince Harry was so impressed by what he saw that he determined to bring a similar event to the UK. Having served in the Army for ten years he knew only too well the type of Serviceman or woman who, their life shattered by a debilitating trauma, finds it difficult to get to grips with the new version of their bodies and minds. To set up a Games event exclusively for those ex-Servicemen and women and veterans would, he believed, help to inspire them and give them and their families a sense of pride and community. The difference between the Warrior Games and the Invictus Games is that the latter involves the families of the athletes who are supported by the Legion to attend. Antony Baines is on the UK board of the Invictus Games. He describes the moment of arrival at a training camp, after dealing with the bureaucracy of the business side of the games: 'It is a world of human resilience and the spirit is magical. To watch a triple amputee throw himself into the swimming pool and get to the other end is humbling. The impact on families is profound. More than one young person has said to me "I've got my Mum back" or "I've got my Dad back."'

While the Games are funded by sponsorship and, until 2019, also by the Ministry of Defence, there are costs and programmes that are borne by others. Help for Heroes assists in recruiting the athletes to represent the UK. After the London Invictus Games in 2014 the charity reported an impressive increase in veterans signing up for sports. Top were those wishing to enrol in powerlifting, a colossal 633 per cent increase

Opposite: Cycling time trials in Sydney, 2018.

Top: 4 x 100m mixed relay.

Above: Britain's Naomi Adie won a silver and two bronze medals in Sydney.

in participation, followed by archery talent assessments with a 463 per cent increase and swimming with 69 per cent more people expressing an interest in taking part. The journey the athletes undertake is remarkable. Training from scratch for two years requires a degree of commitment and determination, often in the face of pain and adversity, that is inspiring.

Meanwhile, the families and carers of the athletes need to be taken into consideration. This group of people is supported by the Legion, which makes it possible for family members to travel to the Games and take part in programmes set up for them while the athletes are training and preparing for the competition. Holly Goodberry is the Legion's Invictus Games Friends and Family Manager for the UK and supports families of Invictus Games athletes not only during the period of the Games themselves but year-round. She has got to know many of them well over the last three years.

> We are around in people's lives for years. There is nothing else out there like it. We know that behind every team member, there are so many people who have helped get them to the start line. A life-changing injury or illness has a huge impact on both the individual and those around them – and we make sure they can be there to cheer them on every step of the way. [24]

Practical help comes in the form of paying for accommodation and tickets, coordinating travel to and from the trials and Games themselves, and providing welfare support. Bearing in mind families come in all ages, there are specially organised tours that can be enjoyed by children, parents and grandparents alike, such as a trip to the Niagara Falls in 2017.

Top: Dave Watson in the shotput at the 2018 Invictus Games in Sydney. He won a gold medal in the discus event and two silvers in rowing.

Above: John Hill's family were supported by the Royal British to see him compete in the Invictus Games.

KELLY GANFIELD

Kelly Ganfield took part in the Invictus Games in Toronto in 2017 and in Sydney in 2018. She enrolled in the British Army in October 1998, signing the Oath of Allegiance less than a week after her 18th birthday. She served as a military clerk in Northern Ireland (Portadown and Omagh) and then in Chester where she played football for the Chester Ladies' Team. In 2001 she became unwell and doctors concluded she had had a stroke after her eyesight began to deteriorate, and eventually diagnosed antiphospholipid syndrome, a disorder of the immune system that causes an increased risk of blood clots. She was 23 years old and registered blind.

She applied to compete in the Invictus Games and was selected to represent Britain in Toronto in 2017. She ran 100m, 200m and took part in the indoor rowing challenge. 'The most wonderful thing about doing the Invictus Games was to represent my country again. I never thought I would ever be given that chance.'

The Legion paid for Kelly's wife, Sarah, to join her in Canada. Their two-year old daughter, Bethany, was also included in the Ganfield party,

as were her parents-in-law. Although Kelly was focused on her competitions, she managed to have one day off and spent it with her family visiting the Niagara Falls. 'Grateful doesn't cover it,' Kelly said when speaking about how she felt towards the Legion.

'My parents-in-law said I was a completely different person from what I was before the Games.' The following year Kelly went to Sydney with Sarah. There she became the first visually impaired athlete to win a silver medal in the 100m relay.

SPENCER BULL

When Spencer Bull wrote to the headmasters of his teenage sons' schools to ask permission for them to have leave of absence to attend the Invictus Games in Sydney in 2018 the reaction was immediate. 'Too right they are going!' was the gist of the response he received from each.

Spencer had already been to the Warrior Games in Chicago in 2017 but this did not involve his family so his wife, Sally, and his three sons had only seen photographs. In Sydney, the families were right in the mix, thanks to the involvement of the Royal British Legion. 'It was a real family and friends event,' Spencer explained. 'The Legion paid for my family's travel and accommodation, while my sister and mother came independently. I realised that it was more important for the family than it was for me in many ways.'

Spencer suffers from multiple sclerosis and was discharged from the Army in 2017. The Army accommodated him as he gradually became more restricted in what he could physically achieve and from 2012 he commanded the Personnel Recovery Unit in Shrewsbury, which deals with WIS who need specialist help and support.

He felt the Invictus Games was a way to say a heartfelt thank you to his and other Service families. 'When events were taking place,' he said, 'you could hear what it meant to them to be there, watching and cheering.' Today he continues to volunteer for charities, and he gives talks in schools, which is something he really enjoys. 'Believe, Engage, Achieve. That is what I want to tell people, to inspire them and encourage actively listening, rather than simply broadcasting and offering advice.'

ART AND THEATRE

While sport is a major driver for regaining confidence and focus for many ex-Service personnel and veterans, the arts can play a significant role in rehabilitation. One ambitious project involved putting on a play, created by wounded, injured and sick (WIS) Service personnel at the National Theatre in London for a gala audience from the world of entertainment in January 2012. Theatre producer Alice Driver had the idea of using theatre as an inspiring method for recovery. She had previously worked with young people in hospitals, hostels and hospices, and had been inspired by the positive impact that theatre has on individuals, whatever their experience or background. A surgeon at the Queen

Elizabeth Hospital Birmingham introduced her to Service personnel who were undergoing treatment following injuries sustained in Afghanistan. She was particularly moved by one patient who said to her: 'When you become wounded, you become incredibly vulnerable, you lose yourself, your identity and fundamentally, you lose your voice.' She knew that she had the ability to help injured Servicemen and women refind that voice. She set up The Drive Project, which uses the power of the arts as a recovery tool for those who have experienced trauma. This was the first time that the Ministry of Defence had stepped away from the safe, known areas of sport and adventurous training and into the world of theatre and art.

With the support of the MOD's Defence Recovery Capability and the Legion, and working with the Theatre Royal Haymarket Masterclass Trust, 32 WIS ex-serving personnel came together to form a theatre company, Bravo 22 Company, under the patronage of Trevor Nunn and General Sir David Richards. The aim was to tell the stories of individual soldiers from their own perspective of their lives before and after life-changing injuries. The result was *The Two Worlds of Charlie F*, written by Owen Sheers and directed by Stephen Rayne but written in the voices of the participants. Sheers wove the individual stories into a play that is raw and shocking, laugh-out-loud funny and deeply moving. He did not seek to tone down the language of the soldiers, nor did he shrink from confronting the audience with the shocking reality of the lives of those severely injured during their Service. The play is set at the time of Afghanistan and most of the cast were under 40. Some had visible injuries – missing limbs or severe limps – but there

Below: In the Art in Recovery programme participants created life-size sculptures over a four-week programme, telling their story of recovery, from injuries, to painful memories, to worries about civilian life.

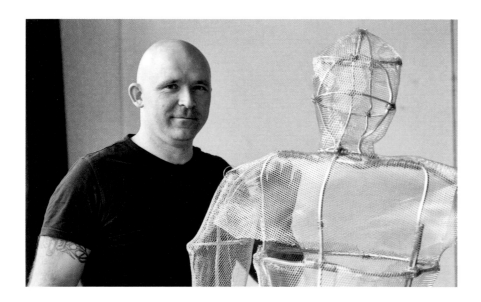

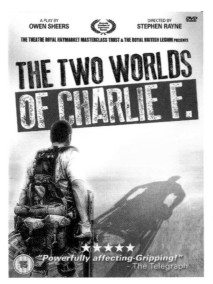

were others, like Colonel Stewart Hill, who suffered a brain injury in 2009 that changed his life but not his outward appearance.

The Two Worlds of Charlie F was planned to be shown on one night only in January 2012 but the reaction to the play was so positive that Masterclass and the Royal British Legion helped to set up a tour of theatres around the UK and Canada. Over the course of 2014 it was shown in 14 theatres between February and June and seen by thousands of people. It received rave reviews and standing ovations everywhere. The play won the Amnesty International Freedom of Expression Award after playing to sell-out houses at the Edinburgh Festival. Its power was in the honesty and authenticity of the voices and stories of the soldier characters and it had a profound

impact on audiences, both military and civilian, bringing the experience of the battlefield to life on stage in a way that no other play has ever done. For Corporal (retired) Steve Shaw it was a wholly positive experience to be part of Bravo 22: 'I got to share my story ... I am convinced no matter the state of mind I may have due to my pain or disability, I know that I am not alone.'

The Battle Back Centre and Bravo 22 are high-profile parts of the Legion's portfolio; however, they represent but a tiny percentage of the work that it undertakes year in, year out. The main part of the welfare work today involves helping ex-Service personnel to cope with the trials of everyday life. In the 1920s it helped destitute families with a bucket of coal, food vouchers and clothing. Today it provides crisis grants for food,

heating and a roof over people's heads, but also vital information, guidance and advocacy. 'In some ways, little has changed,' said Nicola Cook, Assistant Director of Operations for the Legion. 'The basic human needs are still there. We see the challenges that face people leaving the Forces and struggling to cope with life.' She pointed out that those who seek help today are often in their twenties, having served for a few years, and in some ways mirror those men and women who sought help 100 years ago.

One of the things the Legion does successfully is to assess people's needs and pinpoint the main problem facing the individual or family. The teams around the country have expertise in tracking down the right services for those who seek help and often are able to turn someone's life around. In some cases, they profoundly change people's lives for the better. Nicola Cook said: 'It is humbling and inspiring to see the difference we make to people's lives. There are certainly some who we have helped who would not be here but for the Legion.'

Recently the Legion has significantly increased its overseas work. In 2019 tropical storms wrought havoc and destruction on the Fijian islands, from where the Armed Forces recruit men and women. The Legion stepped in to help with rebuilding homes and in one instance gave £3,000 to a farmer who lost everything in the storms to purchase pineapple plants. These types of grants form a vital part of its work and although they are not as eye-catching as the larger projects, they are the backbone of what the Legion offers to those who need its help.

In 2019 the Legion organised an immensely successful and high-profile week-long cruise aboard the MV *Boudicca* to mark the 75th anniversary of

WE ARE THE LEGION

Opposite: The Art in Recovery programme helped men like Steve Shaw, injured in the course of Service, to learn new skills and improve their mental well-being.

Below, left: The tools of the trade.

Below, right: Dennis Callaghan took part in the Art in Recovery programme in Liverpool in 2019.

the D-Day landings. Aboard were 255 veterans, joined by family members and almost 50 care specialist and medical staff for the trip. A further 100 veterans had applied to join but were not fit enough for the cruise, although 30 were able to travel by coach to Normandy to take part in the commemorations. Most of the others were taken to the Arboretum to share the experience on large video screens set up for the event. Ted Cordery, who was a 19-year-old Leading Seaman Torpedoman aboard HMS *Belfast* on 6 June 1944, was one of the veterans who travelled on the MV *Boudicca*. He spoke of the emotional impact of the trip: 'You are going back to bad times. People always say, "We were victorious, we won this and we won that", but at what cost was it won? That's what we remember. I get quite tearful but I'm so grateful to the Legion for including me.'

For the Legion staff who were assisting on the trip, one of the biggest shocks was the number of men who came aboard without luggage. When they enquired as to who had their suitcases the veterans told them that they had only the clothes they were travelling in. It turned out that many lived in isolation and were not affiliated to Regimental Associations nor had they been able to call on the support of others. For some it was the first contact they had had with the Royal British Legion. Today these men are on the Legion's radar and it will continue to make contact with them and check up on their welfare needs. It proved once again that the work of the Legion is not over, but it also shows the need to reach into the community to ensure that no one who is eligible for help slips through the net.

CONCLUSION

The Royal British Legion enters its second century with the same three basic tenets at its core as it had in 1921: the well-being of the Armed Forces community; campaigning on that community's behalf; and Remembrance. It is at once sobering and reassuring to reflect that 100 years after its founding, these principles are still key. The early pioneers, led by Earl Haig and Fred Lister, had the foresight to understand what the Legion would have to offer not just in the immediate future but in the long term. They also understood the importance of bringing the public with them and keeping the government of the day in tune with what the Armed Forces community needed. That still applies today.

Although large showcase events keep the Legion in the public's eye, it is the day-to-day services that it delivers on the ground, in the community, that are at the heart of its work. Men and women who have served the country are at the core of the Legion's welfare programmes, whether that be those who have recently left the Services or veterans who served in the Second World War. The latter are an ageing generation who have multiple and challenging needs. The Legion works in partnership with Dementia UK to deliver the Admiral Nurses service. Admiral Nurses provide help that can offer both practical and emotional support

and are focused on the challenging needs of ageing beneficiaries. These nurses are a lifeline, and they bring hope to those who feel abandoned as they try to care for a family member with dementia.

The issues presented to the front-line welfare teams can be complex and demanding, requiring the skills of those who can untangle a range of issues that might include debt, housing and homelessness, addiction, abuse, immigration questions and the challenges of living independently. These are not headline-grabbing, but they have always been and will continue to be at the centre of what the Legion does. The role of the branches is as important as ever in keeping the Legion's officers up to date with what is happening away from its headquarters, in the towns and villages around the country and further afield, in Commonwealth and other countries worldwide.

The challenge for the future will be to ensure that the Legion's membership and the volunteers, who bring such value to the welfare work of the organisation, are helped to meet those needs. The Legion is part of a much wider network that supports the Armed Forces, but it is also at the heart of the network of military charities, of which there are more than 1,500 UK wide. Annually the Legion spends more on welfare than the next four largest military charities combined

As part of its D-Day 75 commemorative events, the Legion set sail for a week with 255 veterans aboard a specially chartered ship, the MV *Boudicca*, returning to the beaches where many of them landed three-quarters of a century earlier. It was a time of celebration but also of sadness as the veterans remembered those who had not come home. Les Hammond, who landed at Juno Beach in 1944, summed up the feelings of many when he said: 'I'm not a hero. I served with men who were. I'm very lucky. I'm a survivor.'

and has learned that the greatest value it can bring is understanding what it can help others to deliver rather than trying to cover all services itself.

Since the 1990s the Legion has tried to gain a better understanding of the profile of the Armed Forces community. Two broad-ranging household surveys yielded valuable insights which enabled more relevant assistance to be offered to an ever-changing set of needs. The Legion's standing with parliamentarians, government and the Ministry of Defence is one of its most valuable assets and it will continue to lobby on behalf of the Armed Forces. In the past the Legion relied on friends in Parliament but today it is a professional lobbying organisation respected by politicians of every stripe. No one can predict what campaigns will be run in the future, but the Legion has proven successful over the last century in representing the needs of the Armed Forces community. It will continue to shape government support and its own services in the future through its reviews of that community. Crucial to these efforts was the successful Count Them In campaign to include a question on veteran status in the 2021 national census. This will provide, for the first time, accurate information about the location and composition of the Armed Forces community, allowing the Legion to improve its services and campaigns.

The Legion's story is a global story. For more than a century the British Armed Forces have been supported by men and women from all over the Commonwealth and further afield. This is a proud tradition that has a distinguished record in this country. As Lord Gadhia said when he launched the khadi poppy in 2017, 'we have a shared history in Britain, and it is up to us to pass on the mantle to the next generations'. At the

Opposite and below: GP90 was a pilgrimage organised by the Legion in 2018 to mark the 90th anniversary of the Great Pilgrimage when 11,000 veterans, widows and Legionnaires visited the battlefields of the Somme and the Ypres Salient.

Overleaf: For GP90, 1,100 Standard Bearers, each representing ten pilgrims from 1928, led the procession in Ypres.

core of the Legion's DNA is a commitment to loyalty to community, crown and nation. This draws on the values and virtues of military service that the first National Chairman, Fred Lister, defined in his speech at the Unity Conference of 1921 when he spoke of 'Service not Self'. The Legion's current Director General, Charles Byrne, summed up the responsibility today: 'We remember and commemorate the hugely significant events that shaped our identity and our history so profoundly. We continue to work to deliver our core purpose on Remembrance and to our Armed Forces community. We are an organisation with worldwide reach and that ability to look beyond our shores makes us global citizens.'

Looking to the future, the Legion has much to do to adapt to changing times. One of its most public roles is in leading Remembrance. The aim is to ensure that Remembrance belongs to the whole UK population and that it is a source of pride and inspiration across society, bringing in younger and more diverse audiences. The Legion is committed to encouraging this and to bridging the gap between generations and communities. It aspires to broaden the reach of Remembrance by reaching out to the Commonwealth, whose contribution to both world wars and to subsequent conflicts is so vital to the history of our country.

The Legion has always had the ability to sense how commemoration works for the time. This comes in part from the passion of the people behind the organisation who are constantly asking themselves how to keep the Legion's part in Remembrance relevant. Events evolve rather than being shaped and nowhere was this more successful than in the magnificent tribute to the Great Pilgrimage of 1928, which was marked by the Grand Pilgrimage 90 (GP90) in 2018. Exactly 90 years after the first great event, thousands of Legion representatives recreated the Battlefields Pilgrimage visiting the Somme and Passchendaele, walking through the remaining trench systems, as their predecessors had done, and reflecting on the great battles of the past.

On 8 August 2018, they gathered in Ypres Market Square to watch the parade and the One Hundred Days ceremony to commemorate the last 100 days of the First World War. Some 1,100 Standard Bearers and the same number of wreath layers, each representing ten of the original 11,000 pilgrims, paraded through the streets and past the Cloth Hall to the Menin Gate Memorial for the service. As they entered the

impressive memorial, they passed by walls where the names recorded told the story of the many nations from the Commonwealth who stood by Britain's side on the Western Front. The service included an address from the Archbishop of York, whose predecessor had spoken at the service 90 years before, and a message from Her Majesty The Queen.

A poppy petal fall added a moving tribute during Last Post and the Two Minute Silence, followed by the laying of the wreaths. Each wreath had a message from schoolchildren providing a link between the past and the future. Judith Reay, Cumberland and Westmorland's Wreath Layer, said: 'I feel totally overwhelmed and humbled by the whole experience. Making this pilgrimage to the battlefields highlights the sacrifice of millions of Servicemen and women and the great debt we owe each and every one of them. I feel honoured to have been part of this once-in-a-lifetime event.'

This event was every bit as successful for the membership as it had been 90 years earlier and it set a fresh tone for contemporary commemorations. The years 2019 and 2020 presented the Legion with a unique challenge. So soon after marking the centenary of the end of the First World War, which had no surviving veterans, it needed rapidly to meet national expectations for the 75th anniversary of D-Day (6 June 1944) and the end of the Second World War in 2020, where members of that generation are very much with us.

D-Day 75 was an outstanding highlight that saw a seven-day pilgrimage with Fred. Olsen Cruise Lines aboard the MV *Boudicca* around the Channel sites of the Second World War, culminating in a visit to the beaches of Normandy. On board were 255 veterans aged between 91 and 101, joined by 100 more in Normandy where a sculpture made of 20,000 poppies,

Her Majesty The Queen, 90, lays a wreath at the Cenotaph for the last time in November 2016. This duty is now undertaken by the Prince of Wales.

each with a message on it, was erected on Sword Beach. On 5 June Her Majesty The Queen and the Prince of Wales attended a National Commemorative Event to mark the 75th anniversary of the D-Day Landings. The event took place on Southsea Common in Portsmouth, from where much of the landing force left for Normandy.

Then came VE Day 75 and VJ Day 75, which had to be completely refashioned in the light of the coronavirus pandemic. VJ Day 75 went ahead at the National Memorial Arboretum on 15 August 2020, attended by the Prince of Wales, the Duchess of Cornwall and the Prime Minister Boris Johnson. Organised by the Legion and broadcast live on the BBC, it marked 75 years since victory in the Far East and the end of the Second World War. The focus of the Remembrance was the commitment and sacrifice of the members of the 14th Army, the 'Forgotten Army', drawn from African nations and undivided India who had volunteered in their millions.

When David Childs set out to create the National Memorial Arboretum, he had in mind the importance of children in the story of Remembrance. This was embraced by the Legion when it took over responsibility for the Arboretum and today school groups make up a large proportion of the visitor numbers. Working with schools, the Legion will continue to expand the Remembrance material it offers for key stages 1 to 4, covering children from the age of 4 to 16. The resources the Legion supplies are engaging, interactive and have been carefully developed in association with its education partners, including the National Literacy Trust. This is a vital part of the Legion's future work. Children are not only the next generation; they are the future champions of Remembrance.

As the Legion adapts over the next years, what it offers will require a renewed focus. The size and nature of the Armed Forces community has changed over the last 100 years. For the first 25 years the focus was exclusively on those who had served in the First World War. After the end of the Second World War the Legion embraced a new generation of veterans and continued to work with men who undertook National Service. Today's cohort of veterans, many of whom saw action in more recent conflicts, are men and women who chose to serve in the Armed Forces. In 1921 the community, including families, widows and orphans was some 20 million people. In the post-Second World War period almost everyone in Britain had either served at some point or was the spouse, sibling or child of someone who had. Today we have a professional Army, Navy and Royal Air Force with a smaller extended community of family and veterans that numbers some 6 million. Although much has changed in the last 100 years, the needs of those who serve or have served are similar and meeting those needs will remain at the heart of what the Legion does.

The Royal British Legion has become part of the fabric of our society. This is something the organisation treasures but never takes for granted. Like the Armed Forces it serves, the Legion depends on the goodwill of the public and to that end it will continue to work hard to ensure that the commitment and long-term ambitions are focused on maintaining what has become an enduring, reliable and mutually supportive relationship. More important than any of the eye-catching initiatives, however, is the Legion's commitment to men and women of the Armed Forces community who are at its heart. Claire Rowcliffe, Director of Fundraising, summed this up: 'We wrap our arms around those who need us.'

Illustrations are entered in *italics*. Principal coverage of a topic is entered in **bold**.

ENDNOTES

Chapter 1, Note 1: Sandbrook, Dominic, *State of Emergency: Britain, 1970–74*, Penguin, 2010, p. 476.

Chapter 2, Note 2: Michael, Moina Belle, *The Miracle Flower: The Story of the Flanders Fields Memorial Poppy*, Dorrance, 1941, p. 21.

Chapter 2, Note 3: https://poppyladymadameguerin.wordpress.com

Chapter 3, Note 4: *Oxford Dictionary of National Biography*.

Chapter 3, Note 5: Extract from 'Our Empire', November 1931, Vol. VII, p. 41.

Chapter 3, Note 6: Morton, H V, *How the Songs Came to Life*, reprinted in the *Journal*, December 1927, p. 149.

Chapter 3, Note 7: Ibid.

Chapter 3, Note 8: The British Legion, *The Story of an Epic Pilgrimage: The Battlefields Pilgrimage, August 1928*, 1928.

Chapter 4, Note 9: Harding, Brian, *Keeping Faith: The History of The Royal British Legion*, Pen & Sword, 2001, p. 71.

Chapter 4, Note 10: Baines, Antony, author interview, 18 August 2020.

Chapter 5, Note 11: Brown, Anthony, *Red for Remembrance: British Legion 1921–71*, William Heinemann Ltd, 1971, p. 56.

Chapter 5, Note 12: Johnson, Mark, *Caribbean Volunteers at War: The Forgotten Story of the RAF's 'Tuskegee Airmen'*, Pen & Sword, 2014, p. 44.

Chapter 5, Note 13: Ibid, pp. 68–9.

Chapter 5, Note 14: Bashall, James, author interview, May 2020.

Chapter 6, Note 15: Hansard, Cohen's Bill to repeal Section Five of the War Pensions Act, 1921 House of Commons, 21 June 1931.

Chapter 7, Note 16: Harding, Brian, *Keeping Faith: The History of The Royal British Legion*, Pen & Sword, 2001, p. 142.

Chapter 7, Note 17: Ibid, p. 153.

Chapter 7, Note 18: Ibid, p. 157.

Chapter 7, Note 19: Childs, David, *Growing Remembrance: The Story of the National Memorial Arboretum*, Pen & Sword, 2011, p. 2.

Chapter 7, Note 20: Ibid, p. 10.

Chapter 7, Note 21: Ibid, p. 11.

Chapter 8, Note 22: Lake-Bullen, Richard, author interview, 15 April 2020.

Chapter 8, Note 23: Joynson, Chris, author correspondance, 9 April 2020.

Chapter 8, Note 24: Goodberry, Holly, author interview, 18 March 2020.

Images are courtesy of the following contributors. While every effort has been made to contact copyright-holders of illustrations, the publishers would be grateful for information about any illustrations they have been unable to trace. t=top, b=bottom, c=centre, l=left, r=right

Howard Aiken: 160. **Alamy Stock Photo**: PA Images 11, 29, 30, 79r; Stephen Barnes/ Military 15; Colin Waters 19t; World History Archive 19b, 92l; Chris Dorney 31b; M&N 38l; sjcovers 39r; BNA Photographic 61tr; Jeff Gilbert 80; PjrTravel 81tr; Gary Calton 81bl; Dave Porter 85; Rod Varley 92tr; The History Emporium 92br; John Frost Newspapers 93l; De Luan 94l; The D L Archive Collection 94r; Pictorial Press Ltd 97l; Guy Corbishley 109r; Chronicle 110, 165l; Jon D 118; chrispictures 122tr; Benjamin John 122bl; REUTERS 122br; Clynt Garnham/Stockimo 150tl; Peter Jordan_NE 150tc; geogphotos 150tr; Sam Oaksey 150bl; Tim Whitby 150br; Andrew Spiers 151tl; Washington Imaging 151tc; jackie ellis 151tr; Steve Kydd 151bl; martin berry 151c; Kumar Sriskandan 151bc; Andrew Beck 151br;

Maurice Savage 152r; Historical Images Archive 164; Doug Houghton 165r; Ivy Close Images 166; The Print Collector 172; Mike Goldwater 196r; Keystone Press 197l, 228; Homer Sykes 199; Allan Cash Picture Library 229r; Trinity Mirror/Mirrorpix 231; WENN Rights Ltd 250. **Barnton Community Nursery and Primary School**: 120r. **Mrs J Bashall**: 114r. **Alison Baskerville**: 180–1. **Battle Back Centre**: 216, 219, 220br, 221, 222. **Rod Bedford**: 167c. **Bridgeman Images**: Gift of the Department of Defence, 1918 44; © British Library Board. All Rights Reserved 45t; Lebrecht Authors 45b; Prismatic Pictures 58r; Look and Learn/ Peter Jackson Collection 93r; Verdin Collection 156. **Andy Chaloner**: 99l. **Andy Chaloner/Gavin Kingcome**: 27t, 27br, 47l, 47r, 49l, 50bc, 50br, 51, 59, 63tl, 63tc, 63tr, 63bc, 63br, 64tl, 64bl, 64br, 65tl, 74r, 75tl, 75br, 99r, 100, 101c, 101rc, 101br. **Commonwealth War Graves Commission**: 112t, 152l, 153, 154, 167l. **Dean and Chapter of Westminster**: 95r. **Photograph courtesy of Dorking Museum**: 60bl. **Getty Images**: NurPhoto/ Contributor 13b; Hulton Archive/Stringer 20t; Hulton Deutsch/Contributor 26, 33l, 141l; Hudson/Stringer

28l; Topical Press Agency/ Stringer 31t, 126; Alex Bowie 39l; Bob Thomas/Popperfoto/ Contributor 58l; Max Mumby/ Indigo/ Contributor 76l; Peter Macdiarmid/Staff 84l; Chris Jackson/Staff 84r; Fox Photos/Stringer 96; Popperfoto/Contributor 97r, 101tr; Tim P. Whitby/ Stringer 102l, 102r; R. Wesley/ Stringer 135; Kirby/Stringer 137; Keystone/Stringer 141r, 227l; IWM/Contributor & Courtesy of the West Indian Association of Service Personnel 159l; AFP/Stringer 161; Galerie Bilderwelt/ Contributor 163; Steve Wood/Stringer 197r; Terence Spencer/Contributor 198t; Henri Bureau/Contributor 198b; Tim Graham/ Contributor 202l; Fred Morley/Stringer 230; Paul Thomas/Stringer 232; Tom Jenkins/Contributor 233t. **Peter Hansen, Sammlung Gedenkstätte Buchenwald**: 162. **© Illustrated London News Ltd/Mary Evans**: 186. **Imperial War Museums**: 35 (IWM.Art.IWM PST 4928), 95l (IWM Q 31514), 112b (IWM Q 47901), 124 (Art.IWM PST 13811), 127 (Art.IWM PST 13211), 185 (IWM CO 2215). **Heather Anne Johnson/ Gavin Kingcome**: 34, 42, 46l, 46r, 49r, 50tl, 50tc, 50tr, 50bl, 52, 60br, 61l, 61br, 74l, 75tr, 75bl, 75bc, 88, 108r. **Mark Johnson**: 158, 159r. **Keeping Faith: The History**

of The Royal British Legion by Brian Harding, Pen & Sword, 2001: 18 (from p.9), 23l (from p.70), 28r (from p.178), 55 (from p.136), 60tl (from p.127), 91 (from p.132), 111r (from p.96/IWM), 223 and 225 (from p.82/ IWM). **Mick Latter**: 122tl. **Library of Birmingham**: 22. **By permission of the Lloyd family**: 60tr. **Dr Irfan Malik**: 36–7. **© Mary Evans/Sueddeutsche Zeitung Photo**: 193r. **MoD/ Crown Copyright 2017**: 176. **National Army Museum**: 121r (NAM 1956-02-273-1). **National Memorial Arboretum**: 116, 117, 200, 201, 202r, 203, 204, 207, 209, 212, 213. **© National Portrait Gallery, London**: 20b. **Paralympic Heritage Trust**: 227r. **The Poppy Factory/Gavin Kingcome**: 68–71. **The Poppy Factory Archives**: 4, 53, 56, 57, 106t, 107. **Poppy Paper Production © James Cropper**: 66–7. **Press Association**: 178, 179. **Railton Family Archive**: 128l. **Ian Rank-Broadley**: 210–11. **Royal Albert Hall**: 101l. **Royal British Legion**: 8, 9, 16, 21, 25r, 27bl, 54l, 78, 79l, 87l, 90, 98, 106b, 111l, 120l, 130, 131, 138, 140, 142, 143, 146, 170, 175, 182, 187–92, 193l, 195l, 226t; Matt Alexander 2, 13t, 81tl, 86, 168, 244tl, 244bl, 244br, 247, 248; Mark Allan 10, 14, 87r, 103, 104tl, 104bl, 104br,

119, 244tr, 245, 246, 249; Birkenhead Branch 23r; Alun Callender 237, 240; Michael Clement 148, 149, 169; Charlie Clift endpapers, 82, 83; Theo Cohen 233b, 234, 235, 236; Joanna Crawford 241r; Duncan Elliott 241l; Nathan Gallagher 145; Mike Harrington 144; Sarah Jeynes 104tr; Gavin Kingcome 24, 40, 63bl, 64tc, 64tr, 65tr, 65bl, 65bc, 65br, 72, 73, 157, 167r, 226b; Geraint Lewis 238r, 239; Stephen Morgan 12, 133, 134, 214, 243; Gary Moyes 217, 218, 220l, 220tr; The Poppy Shop 76tl, 76tr, 76bc, 76br, 77; Ollie Smallwood 108l, 109l. **Royal Hospital Chelsea**: 81br. **Shutterstock**: 132; Adrian Brooks 41; ANL 196l. **Julie Summers**: 206. **The Theatre Royal Haymarket Masterclass Trust and the Royal British Legion**: 238l. **TopFoto**: 38r, 48, 62, 113, 114l, 121l, 128r, 173, 193c, 229l; Heritage-Images 32; Pastpix 33r, 54r; EUFD 129. **The Wellcome Collection**: 224.

Andy Chaloner's contributions are in memory of Sue Lardge, a Poppy Seller for over 40 years in Wokingham.

ABOUT THE AUTHOR

Julie Summers is the author of 14 works of non-fiction, including *The Colonel of Tamarkan*, which tells the true story of the Bridge over the River Kwai, and *Remembered*, a history of the Commonwealth War Graves Commission. Her bestselling book *Jambusters* inspired the ITV drama series *Home Fires*, which ran for two seasons in 2015–16 and had a regular television audience of over six million. *Dressed for War*, published in 2020, is in development as a drama series. Julie is a Fellow of the Royal Literary Fund and works part time at St Hilda's College, University of Oxford.

AUTHOR'S ACKNOWLEDGEMENTS

This book was written from start to finish under lockdown in the summer of 2020 so I have been reliant on a large number of people to help out when I had questions about any subject to do with the Royal British Legion. I am grateful to everyone who has kindly given up their time to speak to me or share material that has made this book a richer volume. My thanks go to: Howard Aiken, Duncan Andrews, Antony Baines, Sue Bannister, James Bashall, Karan Bilimoria, Jane Britton, Spencer Bull, Charles Byrne, Andy Chaloner, Peter Cleminson, Una Cleminson, Christine Cobbald, Nicola Cook, Catherine Davies, Leroy Deer, Sue Elliott, Joe Falzon, Jitesh Gadhia, Bob Gamble, Kelly Ganfield, Penny Gluckstein, Holly Goodberry, Fiona Hedges, Samantha Heywood, Stewart Hill, Dan Hodges, Francine Holdgate, Dilys Hooper, David Horsfall, Heather Johnson, Mark Johnson, Peter Jones, Christopher Joynson, Christopher Kay, Paul Knox, Richard Lake-Bullen, Shally Ling, Myfanwy Lloyd, Sarah Lopes, Irfan Malik, Ingram Murray, Lawrence Butler Perks, Laura Pett, Tamsin Purchase, Kabita Rai, Philippa Rawlinson, Anny Reid, Claire Rowcliffe, Gary Ryan, Matthew Seward, Sandra Siegmund, Omaar Singh, Richard Steele, Rohan Subbarao, Jo Taylor, Judith Thorpe, Richard Thorpe, Julie Tomlinson, Janet Warby, Roy Wilson, Peggy Wyatt, Gamiel Yafai, Michael Zambra.

Special and personal thanks go to Robert Lee at the Royal British Legion, who commissioned the book in October 2019, and to Emma Vernalls, also of the Legion, who has been such a support to me over the whole period of research and writing.

ADDITIONAL CAPTIONS

Front and back endpapers: Photographer Charlie Clift captured the tattoos of serving and ex-serving personnel to create the exhibition *Tribute Ink*. These images feature: Beni Qio, Dani Cummings, Michael Bell, Josh Pickman, Tash Kenny and Paul Glazebrook.

p. 2: GP90, 2018.

p. 4: Poppy Factory, Richmond, 1920s.

p. 124: Ministry of Labour poster, 1920.

p. 214: Poppy Appeal Ambassador, 2017, Jodie Older with husband Adam and their daughter. Both serve in the Army.

First published in Great Britain in 2021 by Profile Editions, an imprint of Profile Books Ltd
29 Cloth Fair
London EC1A 7JQ
www.profileeditions.com

Copyright © the Royal British Legion, 2021

1 3 5 7 9 10 8 6 4 2

Printed in Italy by Lego srl

A CIP catalogue record for this book is available from the British Library.

ISBN 978 1 78816 5792

Project Editor: Zoe Antoniou

Design and Art Direction: Caroline Clark

Reprographics: BORN, London

FSC
www.fsc.org
MIX
Paper from responsible sources
FSC® C023419